EVERYDAY GLAMOUR

HORROCKSES FASHIONS FROM ROYALTY TO READY-TO-WEAR

EVERYDAY
HORROCKSES FASHIONS FROM ROYALTY TO READY-TO-WEAR
GLAMOUR

Edited by Scott Schiavone
Foreword by Amber Butchart

SCALA

STYLE NO. G. 172
IM. NO. 4206
PRICE
SIZES 10-16
R.S.P.
STYLE NO. J. 82
IM. 4366 DRESS
HX. 3521 COAT
PRICE
SIZES 10-16
R.S.P.
STYLE NO. J. 59
IM. 4351
PRICE
SIZES 10-16
R.S.P.
STYLE NO. J. 384
IM. 4358
PRICE
SIZES 10-
R.S.P.
STYLE NO. G. 268
IM. NO. 4050
PRICE
SIZES 12-18
R.S.P.

STYLE NO. G.
IM. NO. 4185
PRICE
SIZES. 10-16
R.S.P.
COL. 1
COL. 2
STYLE NO. J. 73.
IM. 5625
PRICE
SIZES. 10-16
R.S.P.
COL. 1

FOREWORD

AMBER BUTCHART

FIG 1. Sunsuit in a printed cotton designed by Alastair Morton, Horrockses Fashions, 1948. The Harris (2003.83).

Horrockses Fashions was a manufacturing success story, and one from which we can learn much today. Born from industrial roots, those at the helm of the company recognised the mood of the post-war world and brought creativity, innovation and a canny understanding that risk-taking – when guided by artistic ambition – could produce something remarkable: clothing that was beautiful, more affordable and unmistakably modern.

Horrockses produced printed cotton dresses that were bright, bold and comfortable, and which still look fresh today. Florals that are painterly as well as pretty. Fun conversational prints. And geometric arrangements in discussion with abstract art. Behind these designs lay a commissioning culture that favoured textile designers and fine artists who brought an understanding of the visual language of modernism into direct dialogue with mass production, celebrating talent both up-and-coming and established, from Pat Albeck when she was studying at the Royal College of Art, to designers such as Lucienne Day and Terence Conran, and artists like Eduardo Paolozzi.

The story of Horrockses sits at the intersection of traditional narratives of post-war Western fashion: on the one side, discussions

FIG 2. A Horrockses Fashions sample sheet, with a 1953 print by Eduardo Paolozzi in the background.

of Christian Dior's New Look and the rebirth of Paris couture after Nazi occupation; on the other, the increasing informality and practicality of ready-to-wear brands. Horrockses Fashions occupies a particularly British space between these poles: embedded in industrial history, borrowing couture silhouettes to offer a more democratised alternative in an age of optimism. The Horrockses' customer was a participant in the post-war project of reinvention: dressing for a summer afternoon, a garden party, dancing – for the hopefulness of a country rebuilding itself after the horrors of war.

What made Horrockses radical is precisely what holds its perennial appeal now: the idea that less expensive clothing could still be beautiful clothing. This was not fast fashion in the disposable sense we understand today; instead, it was priced for quality. Garments were crafted with skill – shrink-resistant, colour-fast, carefully constructed and considered in design – and sold at a price that a secretary, a schoolteacher or a young mother could aspire to, while also being worn by royalty.

As such, there is much we can learn from Horrockses' success in the twenty-first century. The fashion industry continues to wrestle with the issues around aspiration versus access, sustainability versus affordability, and artistic integrity versus commercial reality. Horrockses navigated all of these through the discipline of making good things well, which included supporting designers straight from art school, bridging the divide between the fine and decorative arts, and proving that financial success and creativity need not be in conflict.

This book is a glorious celebration of that conviction, and of the importance of good-quality, locally made products that are built to last. It features exquisite new imagery of the garments themselves alongside a peek into Horrockses' archival design books, reproduced for the first time – an invaluable resource for historians, fashion students and vintage aficionados. It covers a story that includes art, industry, women's histories and post-war Britain: an eloquent tale told in vibrant patterns and crisp cotton cloth.

STYLE NO. J 348
JM. 4362
PRICE
SIZES. 10-16
R.S.P.
col. 1
col. 2

1 INTRODUCTION

CHRISTINE BOYDELL

It was on 3 April 1946 that Horrockses, Crewsdon & Co. presented an inaugural collection of 'Dresses, Hostess Gowns and Beach Wear made from Horrockses Fine Cotton' at its London showroom in Hanover Square, Mayfair. The company had a long and illustrious history. It was founded by John Horrocks (1768–1804) in 1791 in Preston, Lancashire, and produced cotton yarn. It was soon to become the largest manufacturer of cotton cloth and cotton goods in the area (4).

The press reception of this first collection was overwhelmingly positive. The trade magazine *The Drapers' Record* commented: 'We commend these cotton frocks for their superior cut, good colours and unusual designs ... Horrockses, the well-known cotton manufacturers have made clothes history by producing a cotton treated for permanent crispness and having the fresh finish of linen'.[1] The *Evening Standard* fashion correspondent celebrated Horrockses' collection, noting that: 'Styling apart, the most interesting features were the modern designs and colourings, both equal to those usually associated with printed silks and rayons' (5).[2]

The brochure for this first collection emphasised the company's worldwide reputation for quality production and

FIG 3. Yellow cotton day dress with cherries, Horrockses Fashions, *c.*1955. The Harris (1998.30.2).

FIG 4. Invitation to the first Horrockses' fashion show, 1946. Printed on cotton cloth.

stressed the importance of the cotton used and the application of treatments that ensured 'permanent crispness'.[3] The clothes presented were accompanied by hats from Pissot & Pavey and shoes by the Hutton Shoe Company of Northampton, all featuring Horrockses' cotton. The key motivation behind the venture was to promote Horrockses' cotton cloth. It was felt that the production of high-class fashions would help elevate the status of cotton and encourage the purchase of cloth by other clothing manufacturers. In 1947 the fashion venture adopted the brand name 'Horrockses Fashions',[4] and became one of the best-loved ready-to-wear labels of the post-war era.

Horrockses had prior experience of fashion, having manufactured fabrics for many years, selling to home-dressmakers, as well as companies producing clothing. It also had an established clothing subsidiary, R.H. Reynolds Brothers (rebranded as 'Reybro' in the 1940s). However, the Horrockses Fashions' project was on a different level. The intention was to create ready-to-wear garments with couture connotations that would rely for success on quality cloth, printed with exclusive, exciting and colourful patterns, all styled following Parisian and London couture trends. To this end, they employed Olive O'Neill (1902–1989) of Dorville as fashion adviser.

Ideas for the fashion subsidiary originated in the late 1930s, but the onset of the Second World War delayed its launch.

The project was initially led by Leslie Brown (1907–1948) who had a wealth of experience working for British Celanese. He worked alongside a team including two fashion designers (Marta Pirn (1916–1995) and Betty Newmarch (1917–1995)), Jane Edwardes (1887–1950) who was in charge of publicity and Nell Sharp (fl. 1947–59) who ran the sample room and was responsible for costings – crucial in a ready-to-wear business. Horrockses Fashions had its showroom and sample room in Mayfair, which was at the heart of the London fashion world. It had acquired making-up factories in 1945, in Manchester (Ivy Mill) and Congleton (W.H. Cliffe & Sons). It had ready access to cloth from Preston, a huge advantage at a time when it was in short supply, and printing was outsourced to a number of firms in the north-west.

The strategy from the outset was to manufacture mass-produced clothing that had couture connotations. The scale of production and the promotion and retailing of the garments were therefore managed carefully. Following couture practice,

FIG 5. A selection of garments from Horrockses' first fashion show, 1946.

FIG 6. A Horrockses Fashions' summer dress illustrated in *The Ambassador*, no. 10 (1951).

Horrockses Fashions released collections twice a year. The cycle ran from November to April for the Spring/Summer collection and from June to September for the Autumn/Winter collection. Fashions shows were held at Hanover Square in May and October, with separate events for retail buyers and the press. The usual practice was to produce 150 to 160 different styles per season and the aim was to manufacture 1,500 dresses per style. As well as the classic sundresses and boleros, shirtwaisters and evening dresses, the company made separates, beachwear and housecoats.

In order to mask its volume production and to emphasise the notion of exclusivity, Horrockses Fashions promoted its clothing carefully. Garments were advertised in the trade press and in magazines such as *Vogue, The Queen, Harper's Bazaar* and *Vanity Fair* (6, 9). The company used top models of the day, including Barbara Goalen (1921–2002), and its favoured photographer was

FIG 7. Pink dress with tulip print designed by Joyce Badrocke, Horrockses Fashions, 1953. Queen Elizabeth II chose a blue version of this dress for her 1953 Commonwealth tour. The Harris (2001.38).

John French (1907–1966), his characteristic clarity and purity of lighting perfectly suiting the crisp cotton dresses. Horrockses Fashions also offered a 'Specials' service as a means of gaining additional publicity. This involved providing individual fittings of garments from the main collections for valued customers, or occasionally a bespoke design. Customers who enjoyed this service included actresses, fashion journalists and the aristocracy. Particularly valuable was the adoption of Horrockses Fashions by members of the royal family, first the Duchess of Kent (1906–1968) and then Princess Margaret (1930–2002) and Queen Elizabeth II (1926–2022). The latter chose several garments for her 1952/53 Commonwealth tour (7). Horrockses' retail customers were forewarned but not allowed to display the specific models chosen by the Queen until she had worn them on the tour. This encouraged buyers to purchase as many styles as possible

FIG 8. Pink cotton housecoat with continuous white ribbon pattern and multicoloured floral design, Horrockses Fashions, *c.*1947. Textile designed by Alastair Morton. The Harris (2020.17.6).

to ensure they had the same dresses that the Queen wore. The publicity surrounding her choices was extensive, the *Daily Sketch* reporting that 'You can wear royal dresses'.[5] The relationship with the film industry was also important. The company supplied dresses for several films in the 1950s, including the 1951 Royal Performance of *Where No Vultures Fly*, throughout which the lead actress Dinah Sheridan (1920–2012) wore Horrockses Fashions.

The main method of getting garments to customers was by selling directly to retail outlets, which could be department stores, independent shops or multiple chains (10). The company was selective: it limited the number of retailers it supplied in a town or city and rejected shops if it did not feel they were suitable. With some department stores it provided garments in a style or pattern exclusive to the store. The careful approach to publicity and distribution, with the emphasis on quality and exclusivity,

FIG 9. A Harvey Nichols advertisement featuring a Horrockses Fashions' evening dress in a print by Margaret Meades (*Vogue*, April 1949).

FIG 10. List of approved stockist for Horrockses Fashions, 1949. Lancashire Archives (DVC/ACC 7340/Box 24/4/2).

contributed to the popularity of Horrockses Fashions and the practice of women asking retailers for the brand. Some retailers even held back newly arrived Horrockses' garments for valued customers. The market for Horrockses Fashions was international, with its products selling particularly well in Commonwealth countries. The company had manufacturing operations in Canada and Australia.

When Leslie Brown died suddenly in 1948, James Cleveland Belle (1910–1983) took over as Design Director. He had been working as a consultant alongside his role as Director of the Cotton Board's Colour, Design and Style Centre in Manchester. His experience in the promotion of cotton and textile design, his involvement in the formation of the Incorporated Society of London Fashion Designers and his role in organising the textile and fashion content of the *Britain Can Make It* exhibition (held at the Victoria and Albert Museum in 1946) made him a perfect choice for Horrockses Fashions. In 1950 he recruited a third fashion designer, John Tullis (1920–2004), who had trained under the couturier Edward Molyneux (1891–1974), as a response to competition from the increasing number of clothing companies entering the market and to inject some couture know-how into the firm.

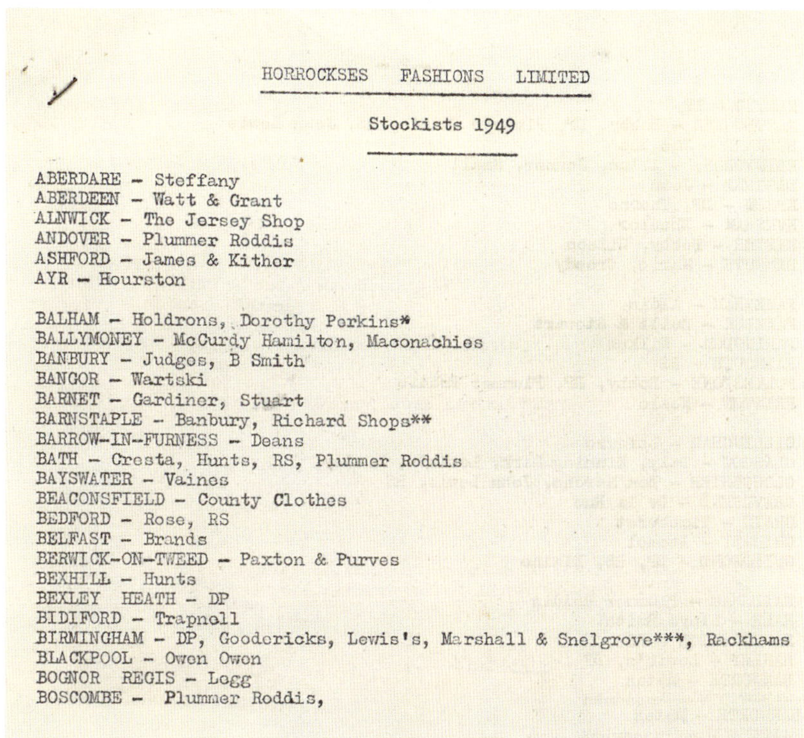

HORROCKSES FASHIONS LIMITED

Stockists 1949

ABERDARE – Steffany
ABERDEEN – Watt & Grant
ALNWICK – The Jersey Shop
ANDOVER – Plummer Roddis
ASHFORD – James & Kither
AYR – Hourston

BALHAM – Holdrons, Dorothy Perkins*
BALLYMONEY – McCurdy Hamilton, Maconachies
BANBURY – Judges, B Smith
BANGOR – Wartski
BARNET – Gardiner, Stuart
BARNSTAPLE – Banbury, Richard Shops**
BARROW-IN-FURNESS – Deans
BATH – Cresta, Hunts, RS, Plummer Roddis
BAYSWATER – Vaines
BEACONSFIELD – County Clothes
BEDFORD – Rose, RS
BELFAST – Brands
BERWICK-ON-TWEED – Paxton & Purves
BEXHILL – Hunts
BEXLEY HEATH – DP
BIDIFORD – Trapnell
BIRMINGHAM – DP, Goodericks, Lewis's, Marshall & Snelgrove***, Rackhams
BLACKPOOL – Owen Owen
BOGNOR REGIS – Logg
BOSCOMBE – Plummer Roddis,

FIG 11. Horrockses Fashions' design book featuring a print by Pat Albeck, Spring/Summer 1954. The Harris (2011.111.2_21).

Cotton was the reason for the existence of Horrockses Fashions and about 85 per cent of its products were made from the parent company's cotton sheeting. The most commonly used quality was 'DGS503', a substantial yet soft fabric exclusive to the Horrockses Fashions' label. In order to stay competitive and to keep the factories in work year-round, Horrockses Fashions also used other fabrics, including rayon jersey, wool, corduroy, silk and nylon. These were bought in from manufacturers such as Sekers. Apart from a few exceptions, most ready-to-wear businesses purchased fabric from a merchant converter who sourced designs and organised for the cloth to be finished. Horrockses, however, retained control of both processes. The only operation to be outsourced was the printing, but this was scrutinised by the firm's technical adviser, Kurt Lowit (1899–1968), who also coordinated the translation of patterns bought in from freelancers. Good, colourful fabric designs were considered a priority. Each collection used 70 to 80 different fabric patterns, but many more were purchased. It was usual to print 7,000–10,000 yards (6,400–9,144 metres) of each design. Initially, designs were produced in the parent company's design studio in Preston, or bought from studios and freelancers. Alastair Morton (1910–1963), the Design Director of Edinburgh Weavers, was a key figure in Horrockses' early success. From 1947 to the early 1950s he was paid a retainer to supply around 40 designs a year. These were characterised by loosely drawn flowers and abstract designs in bright colours (8).

Belle was a frequent visitor to art schools, looking for new talent. At the Royal College of Art (RCA) in 1950 he spotted Joyce Badrocke (1926–2020), who went on to work for Horrockses Fashions in its London headquarters from 1950 to 1957. Patricia 'Pat' Albeck (1930–2017) spent alternate months at Horrockses while still at the RCA and was employed full-time when she graduated in 1953. She worked closely with the fashion designers, producing a varied range of patterns from florals and fruits to her more outrageous lobster print (11, 12). Margaret Meades (1925–2014) was a student at Manchester School of Art and Belle recognised her talent for fine flower drawing, which he felt would be well suited to the production of fashion fabrics. Like Morton, she was paid a monthly retainer to supply designs (5).

One of Belle's tasks at the Colour, Design and Style Centre was to organise exhibitions that introduced manufacturers to new designers. In 1941 he had curated *Design for Textiles by Fine Artists*, which included work by John Piper (1903–1992) and Graham Sutherland (1903–1980). This experience led him to approach a number of well-known painters to design for Horrockses Fashions. Design ideas were bought from Sutherland and Louis le Brocquy (1916–2012) and translated into repeating patterns by the company's own studio staff. In 1953 Horrockses

FIG 12. Horrockses Fashions' design book featuring a print by Pat Albeck, Spring/Summer 1954. The Harris (2011.111.2_21).

FIG 13. Yellow-and-black cotton cocktail dress in a print by Eduardo Paolozzi, Horrockses Fashions, 1953. The Harris (2003.81).

purchased a painting by Eduardo Paolozzi (1924–2005) from the exhibition *Painting into Textiles*, which was translated into a dramatic two-colour design printed on white cotton (13). Over the years, thousands of designs were acquired from studios and freelance designers, including Brigitte Dehnert (1926–1981), Terence Conran (1931–2020) and Lucienne Day (1917–2010).

The establishment of Horrockses Fashions in 1946 was timely. There was a real appetite for fashionable, colourful ready-to-wear garments as Britain emerged from the war. The introduction of more feminine fashions, spurred on by the launch of Christian Dior's 'New Look' in 1947, suited perfectly Horrockses' crisp cotton fabrics, and the company was at the forefront of raising the reputation of what had been considered a fairly lowly material.

Horrockses Fashions' products were relatively expensive. The prices were comparable to other labels such as Linzi and Sambo, but were more expensive than Marks and Spencer and C&A. A classic summer dress retailed for between £4 and £7 and an evening dress from £7 to £16. Such prices suggest that the typical consumer might have been a reasonably well-off middle-class woman – indeed, such women probably made up a large part of the company's customer base. However, many less well-off women were also keen to purchase a Horrockses Fashions' garment. So, they scrimped and saved, maybe buying one dress for a special occasion. They were motivated by the quality of the cloth and its manufacture, the fabric designs and the styling.

We associate the Horrockses Fashions' brand with the 1940s and 1950s, the period during which it enjoyed the greatest success. By the late 1950s British cotton firms were facing increasing competition from the Far East, which resulted in the parent company instigating various cost-cutting strategies, including a reduction in the quality of the cotton cloth. This led to the resignation of several of the key figures who had played important roles in the company's success, including Belle, Lowit and Albeck. Horrockses Fashions was sold to Steinberg & Sons in 1964, which secured a Royal Warrant for the label in the same year. In spite of this coup and the fact that Queen Elizabeth II continued to wear Horrockses Fashions into the 1970s, the success of the 1940s and 1950s seemed a distant memory. Cotton, the *raison d'être* behind the brand, was being overtaken by synthetic fibres. The firm gave up its control of fabric design and began to buy in finished fabrics. It eventually transferred clothing production to the Far East;

FIG 14. Rayon day dress with blue, purple and green printed floral design, Horrockses Fashions, *c.*1947. The Harris (2010.173).

it ceased production in 1983. In recent years there have been various attempts to revive the brand, notably with the Manchester-based Joanie Clothing.

On this 80th anniversary of the founding of Horrockses Fashions, 16 years since the publication of *Horrockses Fashions: Off-the-Peg Style in the '40s and '50s*,[6] we are ready for a fresh look at the label. *Everyday Glamour: Horrockses Fashions from Royalty to Ready-to-Wear* brings together a series of chapters that examine Horrockses Fashions from multiple perspectives, expanding understanding of the brand within the contexts of fashion history, material culture, design and collecting. Together, they provide new perspectives on Horrockses Fashions by connecting the brand to broader themes such as post-war culture, femininity, royal influence, couture translation, museum collecting and contemporary vintage culture. Also, for the first time, rare archival material including Horrockses' design books and sample sheets are reproduced, showcasing the design process from sketch to finished garment. This publication moves beyond a simple brand history, presenting Horrockses as a key case study in mid-twentieth-century British fashion, design and cultural identity.

2 FROM MILL TO MUSEUM
The Creation of a Collection

SCOTT SCHIAVONE

FIG 15. Blue-and-white-striped cotton dress, Horrockses Fashions, *c.*1946–50. The Harris (1977.79.2).

Horrockses Fashions, launched in 1946 as the ready-to-wear division of Horrockses, Crewdson & Co., is one of Preston's most storied cotton manufacturers. The parent company, founded in 1791, had long been a pillar of the Lancashire textile trade, producing printed cottons exported across the British Empire. Seeking to diversify in the face of wartime austerity, the company introduced a line of fashionable, machine-washable cotton dresses aimed at middle-class women.

From the outset, Horrockses Fashions combined industrial innovation with couture flair, commissioning prints from leading textile designers and gaining retail placement in the UK's most prestigious department stores. Yet despite its success, Horrockses remained rooted in Preston. Local pride in the brand's achievements ran deep, and its story was seen as a point of cultural significance in a town built on the rhythms of the cotton trade.

The collection of Horrockses Fashions' dresses held at The Harris Museum in Preston is one of the most significant holdings of its kind in the UK. Celebrated for its vibrant prints, feminine silhouettes and accessible glamour, Horrockses Fashions became synonymous with post-war British optimism. But beyond

FIG 16. The Harris, *c.*1900.

their aesthetic appeal, these dresses embody a rich tapestry of industrial history, female agency and regional pride. This chapter discusses how this iconic fashion collection came to be assembled at The Harris, tracing the transition from private wardrobes to a public archive, and exploring the relationships, decisions and chance encounters that have shaped its growth over the past 50 years.

Cotton and industry: Lancashire and Preston at the heart of the global textile trade

Throughout the eighteenth and nineteenth centuries, Lancashire emerged as the beating heart of Britain's textile industry, with Preston playing a pivotal role in the evolution of cotton manufacturing (17). The mechanisation of spinning and weaving processes transformed the region from a patchwork of domestic makers into a concentrated powerhouse of industrial production. This transformation was driven in part by innovators such as Sir Richard Arkwright (1732–1792), whose development of the water frame and the factory system in nearby Cromford, and later in Lancashire, helped lay the foundation for modern textile manufacturing. Arkwright's model of disciplined, large-scale production was quickly adopted across the county, shaping both the economy and the social fabric of industrial towns like Preston.

The rise of Lancashire's cotton industry, however, was built upon a global structure of colonial exploitation. The raw cotton processed in British mills was cultivated largely on plantations in the American South and the Caribbean, where enslaved Africans were forced to work under inhumane conditions. Lancashire's mills relied on slave-grown cotton throughout the eighteenth and early nineteenth centuries, while manufactured cotton goods were exported to West Africa and used as currency in the purchase of enslaved people, thus perpetuating and profiting from a deeply violent global economy.

Preston's proximity to Liverpool, the principal British slave-trading port, further embedded it within this imperial commercial system. As textile production intensified during the early nineteenth century, Preston became home to large spinning and weaving mills employing thousands of workers, many of whom were women and children. Even after the abolition of the slave trade in 1807 and the emancipation of enslaved people in British colonies in 1833, the mills of Lancashire continued to process cotton grown by enslaved labourers in the American South until the Civil War disrupted supply chains in the 1860s.

Despite these grim foundations, the cotton industry also brought about complex forms of social change within Lancashire. The demands of industrial labour catalysed movements for

FIG 17. *View of Preston from Penwortham Hill*, 1821, by John P. Jenkinson (1790–1821). The Harris.

workers' rights. Preston became known for its radical politics, trade union activity and advocacy for reform. This spirit of progress and creativity would, by the mid-twentieth century, manifest in new forms of textile production, most notably through Horrockses Fashions, which emerged as a leader in high-quality cotton ready-to-wear clothing.

Early collecting and the role of regional museums

Located at the heart of Preston, The Harris stands as one of the finest examples of late Victorian civic architecture in the north-west of England. Conceived as a space for public learning, artistic enrichment and self-improvement, the building was made possible by the bequest of local lawyer and philanthropist Edmund Robert Harris (1804–1877), who left a considerable sum to the city for the establishment of a free public museum, art gallery and library in memory of his father, Reverend Robert Harris (1764–1862), vicar of St George's Church in Preston.

The foundation stone was laid in 1882, and the building officially opened in 1893. Designed by the architect James Hibbert (1831–1903), The Harris reflects the neoclassical style inspired by ancient Greek temples, an aesthetic choice that symbolised its purpose as a 'temple of learning' (16). Its monumental portico, imposing Ionic columns and richly decorated interiors were conceived to embody the values of intellectual and civic pride.

From its inception, The Harris has operated as an integrated institution, combining museum collections, fine and decorative arts, historical artefacts and a public lending library. The museum has played a central role in the cultural and civic life of Preston, offering generations of visitors access to art, knowledge and heritage. It was among the earliest regional institutions to champion contemporary art and design, as well as to collect and exhibit fashion and textiles, a reflection of Preston's historical importance in the cotton industry.

The museum did not immediately collect Horrockses' dresses upon their release, but the cultural climate of the 1970s and 1980s, marked by a growing interest in everyday dress and working women's histories, encouraged curators to reassess their approach. Dresses once regarded as common or too recent began to be recognised as important markers of post-war life. Horrockses' garments, with their accessible glamour and strong Preston ties, were ideally suited to this shift in collecting philosophy.

FIG 18. The Harris's collection of Horrockses Fashions' dresses in the museum store.

FIG 19. Cotton dress with pink roses on a green background and matching jacket, Horrockses Fashions, *c.*1946–50. The Harris (1975.89).

From wardrobe to archive: shaping the Horrockses Fashions' narrative

The Harris's Horrockses Fashions' dress collection grew organically from the community it serves (18). Many of the earliest acquisitions were donated by local women who had worked for the company, modelled in its publicity material or simply worn its dresses to weddings and dances and on seaside holidays. These donations often came with rich personal narratives, recollections of shopping trips, first loves and cherished family photographs, offering invaluable context for the garments themselves.

This community-driven aspect of the collection has become one of its great strengths. Unlike high-fashion garments preserved in elite institutions, these dresses reflect the experiences of everyday women. They tell stories of aspiration and domestic life, of social mobility and industrial pride. They are, quite literally, the fabric of Preston's twentieth-century history.

The foundations of the collection

The Horrockses Fashions' collection at The Harris has grown from modest beginnings into one of the museum's most distinctive strengths. The very first Horrockses Fashions' dress to enter the collection was donated in 1975 (19). The dress and matching jacket are made from a deep green printed cotton, scattered with vivid fuchsia roses. Dating to between 1946 and 1950, it exemplifies the company's signature approach to design: bold, contrasting florals rendered in rich colour palettes that spoke to post-war femininity and optimism.

Just two years later, in 1977, a single donor enriched the collection with three further examples. The first, a black-and-white geometric-printed cotton dress from around 1946–50 (22), features long sleeves, a revere collar and a full, three-quarter-length skirt. The second, again dating to about 1946–50 (15, 21), is a blue-and-white-striped dress with long sleeves, a collar and a similarly voluminous skirt. The third, from 1952, is a tartan cotton dress with cap sleeves and a full, three-quarter-length skirt (20), its lively pattern offsetting the restraint of its simple silhouette. Following these gifts, there was a hiatus of some 13 years before additional Horrockses Fashions' dresses joined the collection.

It is interesting to note that these early acquisitions were unsolicited donations rather than objects actively sought by the museum. In its formative years, the approach to collecting

FIG 20. LEFT: Cotton tartan dress with bow tie, Horrockses Fashions, *c.*1946–50. The Harris (1977.79.3).

FIG 21. BELOW: Blue-and-white-striped cotton dress, Horrockses Fashions, *c.*1952. The Harris (1977.79.2).

FIG 22. RIGHT: Black-and-white cotton dress with a shawl collar, Horrockses Fashions, *c.*1946–50. The Harris (1977.79.1).

FIG 23. Maryse Addison attending a garden party wearing a Horrockses Fashions' dress now in the collection at The Harris (2016.12.14).

Horrockses Fashions' garments appears to have been largely passive. This may, in part, be explained by the curatorial culture of the period, often male-led and predisposed to dismiss fashion as a frivolous or overly feminine field of collecting. Moreover, the garments' relative recency may have worked against them: acquired barely two decades after their creation, they had yet to attain the perceived historical or cultural weight of eighteenth-century dress, with many museums still prioritising nineteenth-century and earlier examples.

By the 1990s, however, attitudes had shifted. The Harris began to actively seek out Horrockses Fashions' garments, supplementing donations with strategic purchases. This change coincided with growing scholarly and public interest in Britain's post-war fashion industry, as well as the broader cultural impact of industrial decline in Preston and across the north-west. With the closure of the last textile mills, the preservation of garments such as these became not only a celebration of design, but also an act of protecting the region's rich manufacturing heritage.

The legacy donation – Maryse Addison

The most significant single donation of Horrockses Fashions' garments entered The Harris's collection in 2016, thanks to the generosity of Maryse Addison (1934–2016). Throughout her life, Maryse was celebrated as one of the best-dressed women in London (23), a reputation no doubt enhanced by a close personal connection to the label: her brother Anthony worked as a designer in the Horrockses Fashions' studio at Hanover Square, London.

Maryse Addison's British father was a highly decorated war hero and her mother was French. A gifted linguist fluent in both French and English, Maryse built an exceptional career in international television and documentary production. She began as a hostess at the 1960 'Eurovision Song Contest' in London before moving to New York with the BBC, where she witnessed history first hand during the assassination of President Kennedy. Returning to London, she produced the BBC's *Europa* series and went on to create acclaimed documentaries across Europe and far beyond. Always impeccably dressed, Maryse combined professional excellence with quiet elegance, often wearing exquisite Horrockses Fashions' garments, many gifted through her brother's work in the design studio, making her a living ambassador for the artistry of British fashion.[1]

FIG 24. Black, white and pink evening dress made from Sekers' nylon, with belt and pink organza bow, Horrockses Fashions, *c.*1955. The Harris (2016.12.18).

Anthony began his career in the 1950s as Personal Assistant to James Cleveland Belle (1910–1983), Design Director of Horrockses Fashions, and quickly proved himself indispensable. His creativity and flair drew him into the heart of the Hanover Square design studio, where he oversaw Horrockses' seasonal publicity fashion shows and acted as the vital link between the Mayfair studio and the factory, ensuring designs translated seamlessly from sketch to finished garment. Maryse became something of a muse and in-house mannequin, and from around the age of 18 she regularly wore dresses either gifted from Horrockses' shows or made especially for her in the studio, tailored precisely to her petite frame. Many of these garments were direct reproductions of

FIG 25. TOP LEFT: Red velvet and satin cocktail dress, Horrockses Fashions, *c.*1956. The Harris (2016.12.1).

FIG 26. TOP RIGHT: Cotton day dress printed with pink roses and white bows, Horrockses Fashions, *c.*1946–49. The Harris (2008.1.07).

couture pieces acquired in Paris with full copying rights. Worn for both work and evening engagements, Maryse's wardrobe from this period, much of it created in the Horrockses' studio, stands as a rare and deeply personal record of the brand's creative peak. When Anthony left Horrockses in the late 1950s, he worked for the London couturier John Cavanagh (1914–2003) where he assisted the designer on the commission of Princess Alexandra's bridal gown for her marriage to Sir Angus James Bruce Ogilvy in 1963.[2]

Maryse's remarkable gift to The Harris comprises 23 Horrockses-related objects, including 17 dresses (24), fabric swatches, accessories and ephemera from the London studio. Alongside the garments, she also donated original paintings by artists who designed textiles for Horrockses, among them a striking work by Graham Sutherland (1903–1980). Further Horrockses' garments and related pieces from her collection, including two couture gowns from the Horrockses' design studio, a yellow Lanvin-Castillo evening dress and a Jean Dessès cocktail dress, were given to Brighton Museum, in the city where she lived. These garments are discussed in more detail in Chapter 7.

The Horrockses Fashions' dresses in her donation range from elegant cotton day dresses to sumptuous silk and rayon evening gowns. One of the most intriguing is an unfinished strapless cocktail dress in deep red cotton velvet with a contrasting pink satin bow and sash down the centre back (25). Left mid-construction, it offers a rare glimpse into the making process, revealing its hidden layers of interfacing, the delicate basting stitches and the craftsmanship that lay beneath Horrockses' polished glamour. Far from being incomplete, this dress stands as a tactile tribute to the artistry, skill and human hands behind one of Britain's most celebrated post-war ready-to-wear fashion houses.

The 'charity shop' dress

One of the most charming and serendipitous acquisitions to enter The Harris's Horrockses Fashions' collection is a lilac cotton dress printed with an elegant design of flowing ribbons and pink roses, their foliage rendered in soft grey (26). The effect is painterly and romantic, typical of the refined yet accessible aesthetic that made Horrockses Fashions a household name in the post-war decades. Its scoop neckline and short capped sleeves are complemented by the characteristically full skirt, creating a harmonious silhouette that balances femininity with everyday wearability.

FIG 27. Strawberry print dress in rayon, 1952. Photograph by Norman Parkinson, British *Vogue* (May 1952).

FIG 28. OPPOSITE: Cotton dress with matching belt with strawberry print on a white background, Horrockses Fashions, *c.*1954. Textile designed by Brigitte Dehnert. The Harris (2024.5).

The story of its acquisition makes the dress all the more special. It was 'rescued' from a charity shop in Preston city centre, where it was priced at just £2.50. The donor, Mrs Karlena Irvine, while browsing, recognised the Horrockses' label instantly and immediately thought of The Harris. Having visited the museum regularly as a child, she recalled spending long periods absorbing the displays of historic fashion and felt compelled to ensure the garment found a permanent home in the very institution that had first nurtured her interest in dress history. Without hesitation, she purchased the dress and brought it directly to the museum so that it could be preserved for future generations.

Such moments illustrate how fortunate The Harris is to have a dedicated and engaged community of supporters who value and champion the preservation of its collections. The continued enthusiasm for the Horrockses Fashions' archive is a testament not only to the cultural importance of the brand but also to the lasting connection the museum has forged with its audiences. Acts of generosity like this underscore the relationship between The Harris and the public it serves, ensuring that treasures, whether purchased from couture salons or charity shops, find their rightful place in the story of British fashion.

A strategic acquisition for the collection

One of the most strategic additions to The Harris's Horrockses Fashions' collection is the celebrated strawberry print dress (28), designed by John Tullis (1920–2004) with a textile print created by Brigitte Dehnert (1926–1981). First introduced in 1952, the strawberry design made its debut in Horrockses' Spring/Summer collection of that year, rendered in rayon (27). It was revived for the Spring/Summer 1954 collection, this time in the company's signature cotton, and was paired with a striking red coat dress, the lining of which carried the same vivid strawberry motif.

The Harris acquired the dress in 2023 from Liz Tregenza. The purchase was a considered curatorial decision, prompted by the museum's existing example of the matching red coat dress with strawberry-print lining (29). Bringing the dress and coat together within the collection reconstituted a complete Horrockses' ensemble, offering a rare opportunity to present the garments as they were originally conceived and marketed.

The dress features a graceful scoop neckline accented with a bow at centre front, short sleeves, and a below-the-knee skirt

FIG 29. Red cotton coat with belt, lined with strawberry print fabric, Horrockses Fashions, *c*.1954. Strawberry print by Brigitte Dehnert. The Harris (2016.12.13).

FIG 30. OPPOSITE: Strawberry print ensemble, *Homes & Gardens* (March 1954), p. 55.

5

6

s are tapered, and the pair on ite page are made from awning- otton denim, with tucks at the front. They are smartest worn igh-necked black sweater or a black shirt. The colour is again in a cravat. *Londonus.*

uffant summer evening dress, cut like a creole's, with a tiered ed skirt and a low neckline; a led scarlet cummerbund ties at The material is one of the popu- airy fabrics of the summer—a ted white organdie. *Susan Small.*

itted princess line is particularly linen—and especially in black he dress, *above right,* is fitted e midriff and has a cleverly- ide, flat band framing the square nd covering the tops of the arms becoming way. *Laeta Ramage.*

y pinks are a feature of the collections. The colour of a ipe strawberry has been chosen ed coat in cotton piqué, over a white poplin printed with life-size ies. The coat is lined with the e full-skirted dress has elbow- eeves and a low, square neck- is beautifully cut. *Horrockses.*

FIG 31. Horrockses Fashions' design book, Spring/Summer 1954. The Harris (2011.111.3_29).

composed of four gored panels to create fullness and movement. Its original belt, still present though slightly discoloured from wear, adds a further note of authenticity.

An illustration of this ensemble was featured in *Homes & Gardens* magazine in March 1954, styled with white gloves and a hat, encapsulating the aspirational elegance of the period (30).

The acquisition is also of particular significance for its association with Brigitte Dehnert, a female freelance textile designer working for Horrockses in the 1950s. While little is known about Dehnert's career, her commission for Horrockses underscores the company's willingness to collaborate flexibly with independent designers, and its progressive approach to supporting creative talent within the post-war British fashion industry.

A Horrockses Fashions' family heirloom

One of the most recent and significant donations to The Harris's Horrockses Fashions' collection is a dress and jacket ensemble designed by John Tullis, first showcased in 1954 (34). The dress is crafted from Horrockses' signature cotton, its crisp white ground enlivened by a refined grey abstract print. The coordinating jacket, in plush black cotton velvet, is lined with the same printed cotton, a hallmark of Horrockses' design practice, lending cohesion and a touch of understated luxury to the ensemble.

The donation reached the museum through the most unassuming of channels: an email sent to The Harris's general enquiries mailbox, later forwarded to the curatorial team for assessment. Its provenance proved irresistible. The ensemble, purchased at Harvey Nichols in London where she worked as a ballroom-dancing teacher, was worn by the donor's mother, Mrs Derek Wells, as her going-away outfit following her wedding on 10 July 1954. The wedding, reported in the local press, not only announced the marriage (she was the daughter of a local Justice of the Peace), but also described the attire in great detail, crediting Horrockses as the designer.

The historical record extends beyond family memory. Preserved in the Horrockses' archive at Lancashire Archives is a cutting from the *Daily Telegraph*, dated 18 March 1954, listing the ensemble as the must-have of the season and pricing it at 17½ guineas, the equivalent to approximately £430 today. The donor further enriched the acquisition with a photograph of her mother wearing the outfit on the couple's honeymoon journey to Cornwall, capturing the dress in the lively context for which it was intended (33).

A further stroke of fortune cemented the curators' decision: the original design and fabric swatch for this very ensemble survive in Tullis's design book, now part of The Harris's own holdings (32).

FIG 32. Horrockses Fashions' design book, Spring/Summer 1954. The Harris (2011.111.3_16).

FIG 33. Mrs Derek Wells (née Helen Maxey Haile) wearing the John Tullis-designed outfit en route to Cornwall for her honeymoon, 1954. With permission from the family.

FIG 34. OPPOSITE: Cotton dress and velvet coat worn as a going-away outfit, Horrockses Fashions, 1954. Designed by John Tullis. The Harris (2025.5).

The convergence of designer archive, personal history and preserved garment offers a rare completeness, allowing the piece to be understood not only as an example of mid-century British fashion but also as a vivid artefact of a moment in time.

Preserving legacies, shaping futures

As the volume of donated Horrockses' garments increased, so too did curatorial understanding of their value, not only as industrial products but also as fashion objects. These garments are now meticulously catalogued, stored in conservation-grade conditions and studied in relation to period catalogues, marketing material and wider fashion trends in post-war British ready-to-wear.

The Horrockses Fashions' collection at The Harris stands today as one of the most important repositories of mid-twentieth-century British fashion, embodying the convergence of industry, artistry and everyday experience. These garments, once worn for weddings, dances, holidays and daily life, now serve as touchstones of design innovation and social history, bridging Preston's industrial past and Britain's post-war fashion culture. They demonstrate how ready-to-wear could be elegant and aspirational, while remaining firmly rooted in the material realities of cotton manufacture.

Looking to the future, the collection offers extraordinary potential. Through ongoing acquisitions, digitisation and innovative interpretation, The Harris is committed to deepening our understanding of Horrockses' role within both regional and national histories of fashion. Ultimately, The Harris's Horrockses Fashions' collection is far more than a record of style; it is a living archive of creativity, resilience and cultural pride. In preserving and expanding this collection, the museum not only protects a remarkable chapter of Preston's heritage and British ready-to-wear, but also ensures its relevance for future generations, positioning fashion as a vital lens through which to understand industry, identity and society itself.

3 TRADITION WITH VISION

LISA MASON

FIG 35. Cotton dress with blue, green and purple leaf and flower pattern with a scoop neckline and large bow tie at the centre front, Horrockses Fashions, *c.*1947. Textile designed by Alistair Morton. The Harris (2020.17.5).

Lancashire is textile country. From mills converted into housing, to structures created from the profits of industry, the signs have been etched into the environment, having ultimately shaped the region. Textile production expanded during a period of rapid industrialisation from the late eighteenth century onwards, and John Horrocks (1768–1804) was one of many industrialists in north-west England capitalising on new technologies and markets. Horrockses, Crewdson & Co. was producing enough cloth to 'wrap around the earth at the equator' according to a promotional booklet published in 1938.[1] The company knew cotton intimately and carried out every stage of the manufacturing process – from the raw material to the finished cloth – at its base in Preston. The brand sought to promote its rich heritage as well as its investment in cutting-edge technology and international reach.

Horrockses, Crewdson & Co. boasted an impressive lineage but needed to adapt to survive in a rapidly changing world. In the years leading up to and during the Second World War, the textile and fashion industries had undergone systemic shifts, and the landscape of production and retail had permanently shifted. The Utility Scheme was introduced by the UK government

FIG 36. Horrockses Fashions' fabric design book showing a variety of floral and abstract print designs, *c.*1959–60 (pp. 2 and 3). Lancashire Archives.

in 1941 in response to wartime material shortages, aiming to make the production of civilian clothing more efficient and provide consumers with better-quality clothing. The North American fashion industry also had a major impact in the UK, which introduced standardised sizing and adopted US systems of garment production that became influential in the context of an increasingly globalised industry.[2] These developments would ultimately shape how the industry was organised in the post-war period.

In response, parent company Horrockses, Crewdson & Co. launched the subsidiary Horrockses Fashions in 1946, which designed and manufactured ready-to-wear garments constructed primarily from Horrockses' cotton cloth. By entering into the high-end ready-to-wear field, the company could ensure a steady and controlled market for its product, but it evolved into so much more, creating well-designed, quality garments, featuring innovative textiles designed exclusively for the company by exciting young designers and artists (36).

Christine Boydell, in her seminal publication on Horrockses Fashions, quotes *Vogue* editor Audrey Withers from an essay in the catalogue of the 1946 exhibition *Britain Can Make It*, in which she states that the textile is 'the raw material' of the fashion designer's craft.[3] In the same essay, Withers advocates for a closer relationship between the interrelated spheres of fashion and textile design. The exhibition opened to the public the same year that Horrockses Fashions launched, and the newly minted ready-to-wear enterprise embodied this principle. The reception

FIG 37. Advertising material from the 1950s promoting the Quintafix finish, developed in association with the Bradford Dyers' Association. The Harris (2011.122).

of Horrockses Fashions' inaugural collection was overwhelmingly positive, and the media appeared to be sympathetic to the company's aims:

> Cotton frocks are making a welcome appearance on the summer scene, and enchanting printed cottons at that. Patterns and colours have been completely metamorphosed by the manufacturers during the time that they have been hibernating. The first of the peace-time ranges of cottons shows them stylish as well as incorporating all the technical inventions and finishing processes discovered during the research of war-time.[4]

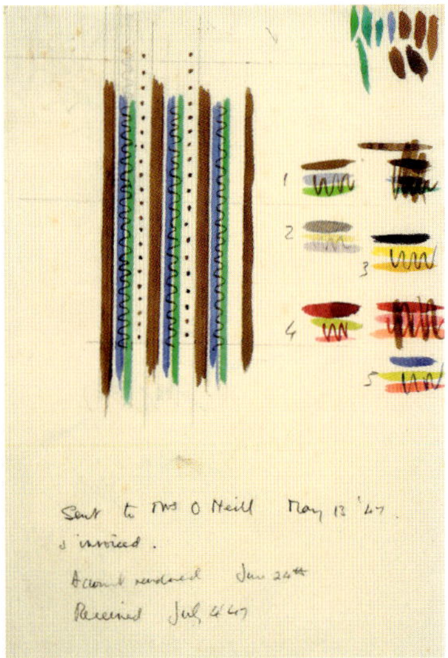

FIG 38. Design for Horrockses by Alastair Morton (AM1), 1947. Gouache and ink on paper. Annotated: 'Sent to Mrs O'Neill, May 13 '47'. This was the first design produced by Morton for Horrockses Fashions and includes five alternative colourways. Abbot Hall, Kendal (Lakeland Arts Trust).

The launch of Horrockses Fashions coincided with cotton becoming accepted as a fashion fabric, in a move away from the fibre's association with hardwearing working dress. Wholesale couture firms such as Dorville, Rahvis and Rose & Blairman were using cotton in their collections by 1946.[5] Newly developed finishing processes rendered these fashionable cotton garments crisp, shrink-resistant and colourfast. Horrockses' advertising copy touts its quest for 'permanent crispness'[6] and the adoption of the Quintafix process (37). Textiles were, naturally, a central focus for Horrockses, and the freshness and diversity of its materials received praise from leading fashion commentators such as renowned journalist Alison Settle: 'To Horrockses women owe a deep debt because they caused cotton patterns to grow up and, within the last few years, produced inexpensive cloths of vast distinction.'[7]

On average, Horrockses Fashions 'produced between 150 and 160 styles per season made from 70 to 80 different fabric designs' (36).[8] To remain competitive in a rapidly expanding marketplace, the company had to ensure a steady stream of new textile designs, with a variety of styles to appeal to different tastes, ages and lifestyles. Boydell argues that the company utilised exclusive textile designs to remain competitive and disguise the mass-produced nature of Horrockses' output.[9] The garments themselves were relatively simple in construction, with Paris-influenced designs adapted for the ready-to-wear market and the middle-class consumer. Horrockses Fashions acquired fresh new designs via a number of channels, including in-house designers, freelance designers, purchasing designs from commercial studios and, occasionally, sourcing designs from artists.[10]

FIG 39. White-and-pink cotton day dress with a *toile de Jouy* pattern, Horrockses Fashions, *c.*1948. The Harris (2011.110).

A figure that looms large in the history of Horrockses Fashions is James Cleveland Belle (1910–1983), Design Director from 1948 to 1958. With his creative energy and connections within the fashion and retail sectors, Belle pushed Horrockses 'to the forefront of progressive ready-to-wear design and the use of avant-garde fabrics'.[11] Belle was also the inaugural Director of the Cotton Board's Colour, Design and Style Centre in Manchester and was involved in a number of exhibitions intended to raise the status of cotton as a fashion fabric. At Horrockses Fashions, Belle worked closely with technical adviser Kurt Lowit (1899–1968), a textile chemist who immigrated to Britain from Czechoslovakia in 1939. Lowit was responsible for engaging the numerous firms contracted by Horrockses to print its fabrics, coordinating the translation of fabric designs for printing and overseeing quality control.[12]

FIG 40. Sunsuit in a printed cotton designed by Alastair Morton, Horrockses Fashions, 1948. The Harris (2003.83).

Sourcing innovative designs was an ongoing challenge for Horrockses Fashions, and in 1947 the firm paid visionary artist/designer Alastair Morton (1910–1963) an annual retainer of £750 (then a substantial fee for a freelance designer) to provide at least 40 designs per year (38, 40).[13] Morton was the third generation of a textile manufacturing family, a gifted abstract painter, textile designer and enthusiastic collaborator. He led the firm Edinburgh Weavers – an experimental offshoot of parent company Morton Sundour – which was responsible for producing some of the most ambitious interior textiles of the post-war period. Morton designed printed textiles for Horrockses, exhibiting an innate sense of colour and dynamic composition that was key to the firm's early image. He provided a total of 440 designs for Horrockses during his time as a freelance designer.[14] Indeed, Morton's free-flowing floral and abstract organic designs became synonymous with Horrockses Fashions in the late 1940s and early 1950s.

Textile design has, historically, been a largely anonymous profession in which designers are rarely credited. Additionally, the survival of complete archives is relatively rare, further complicating efforts to understand the human networks behind the textile sector. A window into the industry, from the designer's perspective, can be found in the archives of Horrockses' textile designers Patricia 'Pat' Albeck (1930–2017) and Joyce Badrocke (1926–2020). The assorted press cuttings, textile designs, artworks, student essays and ephemera were carefully collated by the designers themselves and have been entrusted to the Archive of Art & Design at the Victoria and Albert Museum.

It was through the Royal College of Art (RCA), London, that Pat Albeck and Joyce Badrocke came to work for Horrockses Fashions. At the time, it was common practice for progressive firms to recruit young designers directly from art colleges. Creative directors such as James Cleveland Belle and Alastair Morton would regularly attend diploma shows to seek out emerging talents.[15] In the post-war period, the landscape of art and design education began to evolve from exclusively elite to mass education, and grants paid by Local Education Authorities were introduced. Art schools operated largely outside of the university system and learning took place in small institutions located across the UK. Notable exceptions were the Slade School of Art (part of University College London) and the Royal College of Art (which had its origins in the Government School of Design), which sought to more fully integrate theory and practice.[16] Not all higher education establishments practised such enlightened teaching. Serbian-born textile designer Bernat Klein (1922–2014) received a progressive modernist education at the Bezalel Academy of Arts and Design in Jerusalem before relocating to Leeds University to study for a diploma in textile technology in 1945. At Leeds, Klein found the technical aspects of his education comprehensive but the teaching in the principles of design and aesthetics lacking.[17]

Pat Albeck studied at Hull College of Art and the Royal College of Art from 1950 to 1953 (41). It was at the RCA that Belle spotted her burgeoning talent and purchased her designs for Horrockses Fashions, ultimately employing her as a home-based salaried designer.[18] The abundance of design drawings and works on paper in the archive reveals a young designer with undeniable panache, who understood colour relationships and scale, and had mastered a broad vocabulary of design styles. Albeck possessed

FIG 41. This design was purchased from Pat Albeck's 1953 Royal College of Art diploma show and produced by Horrockses Fashions in summer 1953. Screen-printed cotton, graphite on paper, photographic print. The Harris (2011.111.3).

a prodigious appetite for creative risk-taking, and her output includes illustrative botanical forms, small repeating motifs and bold geometric forms.

A particularly striking example is a design of capsicum peppers suspended from bamboo canes, executed in vivid inks and dynamic gestural brushstrokes, employing mark-making economically, rather than rendering the subject matter in precise detail (42, 43).[19] This design was screen-printed onto a full, pleated, crisp white cotton skirt, with the addition of sheaths of sweetcorn in 1956.[20] A comparison of the design and finished garment shows how faithfully Horrockses Fashions translated Albeck's bold brushstrokes and vibrant pops of colour into the finished textile product.

Much of the success of Horrockses Fashions can be attributed to advances in the relatively new medium of screen-printing during the early twentieth century. Prior to this development, roller printing was the predominant method of printing on an industrial scale, but the cost of engraving copper rollers was prohibitively high for shorter runs of fabric, limiting the potential for creative risk-taking.[21] In addition to capturing a rich variety of textures, screen-printing was also a viable choice for more experimental fabrics produced on a smaller scale.

FIGS 42 AND 43. A design of peppers (ink on paper) and the screen-printed design on a white cotton poplin skirt from 1956. Pat Albeck archive (AAD/2004/9/75 and AAD/2004/9/81).

FIG 44. Evening dress in corded cotton with a printed design by Joyce Badrocke, Horrockses Fashions, early 1950s. The Harris (1999.562.2).

FIG 45. OVERLEAF: Joyce Badrocke, textile design for Horrockses Fashions in six colourways, 1953. Screen-printed cotton. Joyce Badrocke archive (AAD/2009/4).

Joyce Badrocke studied at Worthing Art School and was awarded an Exhibition Scholarship to attend the Royal College of Art in 1947 (44, 45).[22] She was also awarded an Industrial Art Bursary by the Royal Society of Arts in the 'Dress Textiles' category in 1949, funding her travel to Paris to view the collections of Edward Molyneux (1891–1974) and Pierre Balmain (1914–1982).[23] Badrocke graduated with a design diploma from the RCA in 1950, and was then required to spend a further nine months working in industry to qualify for her degree. As with Albeck, Belle spotted Badrocke's talent at her RCA diploma show and she would go on to become an in-house designer for Horrockses Fashions.

Badrocke's textile designs include bold geometric prints, delicate painterly florals, irregular stripes and checks, organic forms, and abstracts composed of gestural brushstrokes. A design of ink spots (45) – splashed seemingly at random across cotton poplin – was featured in 'Chosen by Vogue' in January 1953; the design was made into a full-skirted evening dress that retailed at Cresta Silks.[24] Badrocke's delicate, whimsical prints translated particularly well into childrenswear for the Horrockses' 'Pirouette' range, and she also designed graphic material for the company, such as advertisements and showcards.

The Joyce Badrocke archive includes her RCA thesis entitled *Museum Themes in Print Design*, which encouraged designers to look at natural history specimens as inspiration for surface design. In this thesis, she notes:

> the variety of patterns found in rocks, stones, corals, etc., is quite incredible, many of them being exceedingly simple and supposedly modern in feeling. These fossils, stones etc should provide an inexhaustible source of ideas for the designer, and for an unlimited variety of spotted, striped or abstract patterns the abundance found in these natural origins far exceeds anything the artist can create.[25]

Badrocke produced a corresponding series of designs for textiles based on the natural world, adapted to form repeating patterns (46). The approach of closely observing nature and often distilling it to essential elements is evident throughout Badrocke's career at Horrockses Fashions. Her mining of nature, from a scientific perspective, chimes with wider currents within art and design of the period. At this time, scientific imagery – particularly

"Evening News"

Ink Spots

What next? "Ink spots," spattered unevenly all over plain prints, are shown in day and evening dresses.

They spatter a very simple dance

Chosen by "Vogue",
January 1953.

9. Handkerchief-fine full evening dress of white poplin printed with spidery black scrawls and blots, the tightly shirred and shaped bodice looped through with a long velvet-lined scarf. By Horrockses, 9½ gns. from Cresta Silks, Regent Street, Bristol and Brighton

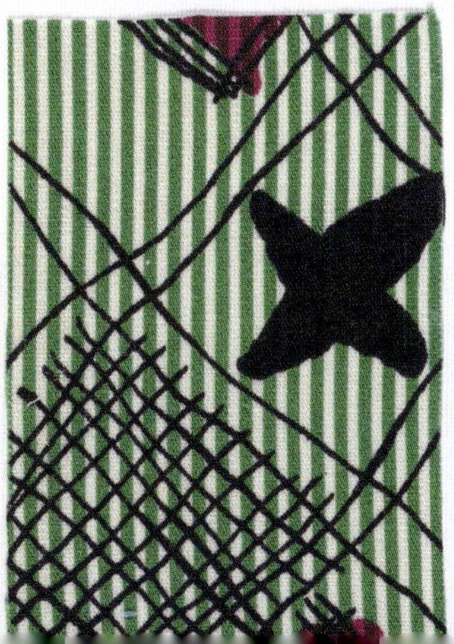

FIG 46. Design on paper with gouache, from Joyce Badrocke's thesis presentation, 1950. Joyce Badrocke archive (AAD/2009/4).

mathematical biology and crystallography – was an important source of inspiration for many forward-looking artists and designers as they challenged artistic hierarchies, seeking to create a visual language fit for the future.

Crystallography was the impetus for surface designs produced by the Festival Pattern Group (47), a collaboration between Dr Helen Megaw (1907–2002) (a leading crystallographer from the Cavendish Laboratory at Cambridge University) and the Council of Industrial Design, to create designs based on X-ray diffraction photographs of crystals and diagrams of atomic structures.[26] These designs were showcased at the Festival of Britain in 1951. Although the group ultimately disbanded, its legacy can be seen in the atomic elements of design prevalent in the 1950s. Alongside the 1951 Festival, the radical Independent Group organised an exhibition entitled *On Growth and Form* at the Institute of Contemporary Arts. Curated by Richard Hamilton (1922–2011), the exhibition sought to 'look inside nature and show the processes, living and dead, by which nature works'.[27] The title was based on the influential publication of the same name by mathematical biologist D'Arcy Wentworth Thompson (1860–1948).

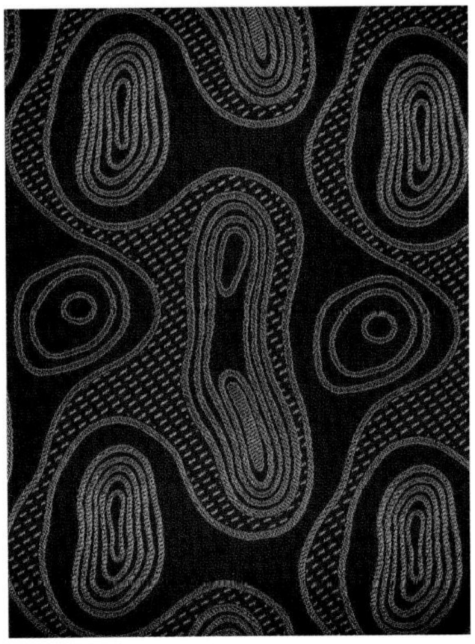

FIG 47. This furnishing textile entitled 'Surrey' was based on the crystal structure of the mineral afwillite and became one of the most successful designs produced by the Festival Pattern Group. Designed by Marianne Straub for Warner & Sons, 1951. Power-woven cotton and rayon.

Horrockses Fashions also sourced textile designs from leading artists. Interestingly, the artists' names do not feature on any of the extant advertising copy. Nonetheless, the designs did generate significant press and placed Horrockses at the centre of a network of progressive firms seeking to unite the spheres of fine and decorative art. *The Ambassador* magazine was a pivotal force in promoting the export interests of the British textile industry (48).[28] Launched in 1940, the magazine operated under the maxim 'Export or Die' and featured some of the most progressive textile designs being produced in Britain. The venture was launched by the German émigré couple Hans (1904–1975) and Elsbeth (1911–2014) Juda, with Elsbeth contributing striking photography to the publication under the pseudonym 'Jay'. *The Ambassador* sought to reinvigorate the industry by advocating for a closer relationship between fine art and textile design. A seminal moment in this movement came in the form of the exhibition *Painting into Textiles*, which was staged at the Institute of Contemporary Arts, London, in 1953. The exhibition's guiding principal was to show works by fine artists that would serve as catalysts for exciting new textile designs. Twenty-five contemporary artists were invited to submit pieces to the exhibition, including Henry Moore (1898–1986), Graham Sutherland (1903–1980) and John Piper (1903–1992). Alongside the work of these artists, 'established and new textile designers' also featured in the exhibition, such as Pat Albeck, Lucienne Day (1917–2010), Marian Mahler (1908–1982) and Jacqueline Groag (1903–1986).[29] In an introductory essay, Hans Juda set forth the aims of the exhibition:

> The Arts are not luxuries, leading gentle lives of grace and piety in a vacuum; they are a strong living force. In a world increasingly critical and increasingly alive to design, all of us are conscious of the need to provide new sources of inspiration which will refresh our ability to produce and sell ... By bringing the artist and the converter into closer communication, trade will be enriched, kept fresh and active.[30]

Horrockses Fashions purchased a painting by Eduardo Paolozzi (1924–2005) from this exhibition, which was translated into a striking screen-printed cotton day dress (49, 50). Paolozzi was a pioneer of pop art and postmodernism who sought inspiration from advertising, media imagery and everyday ephemera.

FIG 48. OPPOSITE: Elsbeth Juda, photograph of Barbara Goalen modelling textiles for Calico Printers' Association board members, Lancashire, for *The Ambassador*, no. 9 (1952), pp. 79–94. Elsbeth Juda archive (AAD/2004/9/81).

FIG 49. RIGHT: The hallmarks of Eduardo Paolozzi's printmaking are evident in this design entitled 'Collaged Elements', including the collage aesthetic, presence of ephemeral objects and quasi-scientific imagery. Designed for David Whitehead Ltd, Lancashire, *c.*1953. Screen-printed rayon. National Museums Scotland (K.2019.63), presented by the Art Fund.

FIG 50. BELOW: Yellow-and-black cotton cocktail dress in a print by Eduardo Paolozzi, Horrockses Fashions, 1953. The Harris (2003.81).

His practice encompassed sculpture, printmaking and collage. He worked collaboratively across different media, creating mosaic murals for Tottenham Court Road underground station and numerous tapestry projects with Archie Brennan (1931–2019) and the Edinburgh Tapestry Company (now Dovecot Studios). Paolozzi was involved in textile and surface design, forming the experimental print collective Hammer Prints with Nigel Henderson (1917–1985) in 1954 and working as a freelance designer for clients such as Wedgwood, David Whitehead Ltd and Lanvin.[31] Paolozzi also taught textile design at the Central School of Arts and Crafts (now Central Saint Martins), London, where he mentored a future generation of emerging designers, including Althea McNish (1924–2020) and Terence Conran (1931–2020).

Another notable artist who created designs for Horrockses was Graham Sutherland. This connection came about through James Cleveland Belle, as he had worked with Sutherland on exhibitions held at the Colour, Design and Style Centre.[32] Sutherland studied engraving and etching at Goldsmiths College, London, and his output flowed between design, printmaking and oil painting. His subject matter was rich and varied, finding expression in highly personal responses to the natural world, and often featuring surreal landscapes and humanoid figures. Sutherland also worked across media, collaborating with the

FIG 51. Design drawing by Daphne Razzle for Style 803 showing the Graham Sutherland design in an alternative colourway, late 1940s. Graphite and textile on paper. Daphne Razzle archive (AAD/2015/11).

FIG 52. OPPOSITE: Cotton shirtwaister dress in a fabric designed by Graham Sutherland, Horrockses Fashions, late 1940s. The Harris (2003.82).

Edinburgh Tapestry Company (now Dovecot Studios) and with Pinton Frères, near Aubusson, France, on the monumental commission *Christ in Glory in the Tetramorph* for the newly rebuilt Coventry Cathedral. Clients for Sutherland's design work included Cole & Son (Wallpapers) Ltd, Ascher (London) Ltd, Warner & Sons, John Heathcoat and Co. Ltd, Helios Ltd, and Cresta Silks Ltd. Florals and semi-abstract biomorphic forms were common elements of Sutherland's designs: a notable furnishing design for Helios was even entitled 'Sutherland Rose'.[33]

One of Sutherland's designs for Horrockses Fashions (51, 52) features bands of biomorphic forms in red on a deep blue ground, reminiscent of his etchings – a fresh take on the banded designs popularised by Alastair Morton. Boydell notes that although some of Sutherland's fabrics for Horrockses were limited to prestige lines, his designs were also used for simple shirtwaisters and sundresses, which were produced 'in quantity'.[34] For artists such as Paolozzi and Sutherland, working within the democratic medium of textile design served an ideological function, challenging established notions between 'high art' and everyday life.

A receptive market was key to the success of the Horrockses Fashions' project. The British government was intimately involved in shaping public taste in the post-war period. Design played a crucial role in the propaganda campaigns of the Second World War and evolved during peacetime to promote Britain's place on the global stage in the face of shifting geopolitics. Rebuilding a solid manufacturing base and sparking economic regeneration through export trade was vital as the country recovered from war. The Council of Industrial Design was formed in 1944 by the Board of Trade, with the stated aim: 'To promote by all practicable means the improvement of design and the products of British industry'.[35] The Council acted on behalf of industry by setting up Design Centres (in London and Glasgow), supporting further education, and serving a somewhat didactic function in educating the British public on the importance of 'good design' via exhibitions and other media. Mounting exhibitions was inherently political, attempting to promote British manufactured goods on the world stage, but these events also functioned as leisure activities for a war-weary public, introducing them to exciting new forms of visual culture. The Council of Industrial Design organised the exhibition *Britain Can Make It* (held at the Victoria and Albert Museum in 1946) and was central to the implementation of the Festival of Britain (organised by Clement Atlee's Labour government and staged across the UK in 1951), a national celebration of science, technology and the arts.[36] These events introduced the British exhibition-going public to the radical abstract organic surface designs of Lucienne Day, Marian Mahler and Jacqueline Groag.

The Festival of Britain was intended to mark the centenary of the Great Exhibition of 1851. The goods showcased at the Great Exhibition acted as a lightning rod for debates around the role of art and design in society, fuelled by paradigm shifts in technology, social mobility and the increasing proliferation of consumer goods, and resulted in calls for design reform. One means of creating a new design vocabulary for British industrially produced goods was by uniting the fields of fine art and industrial design, and progressive firms such as Horrockses Fashions can be seen as embodying this legacy. Although these ideas had been circulating in the early twentieth century – finding expression in experimental design collectives such as the Omega Workshops, the block-printed designs of Phyllis Barron and Dorothy Larcher, Cryséde and Cresta Silks – they gained momentum in the immediate post-war period, as designers and manufacturers looked to the future.[37]

The immediate post-war period saw greater fluidity between fine and decorative art and central to this movement was the Czech émigré couple Lida (1913–1983) and Zika (1910–1992) Ascher (53). Due to Zika's Jewish heritage, they were forced to flee Czechoslovakia in 1939 when their home country was annexed to Germany. They set up their own printworks in west London in 1942. The young company began selling printed fashion textiles designed by Lida to couturiers such as Edward Molyneux and went on to supply fabrics to the major houses of Europe. The couple's ideas were influenced by the *Design for Textiles by Fine Artists* exhibition, staged at the Cotton Board's Colour, Design and Style Centre in 1941, which had been organised by James Cleveland Belle.[38] In 1944 the Aschers launched the 'Artists' Squares' project, inviting artists to design scarves or headsquares, which were produced in limited editions in the Aschers' own printworks. Artists could use any technique and any number of colours within their designs, the only stipulation being that they should measure 90 cm square. The Aschers worked with artists including Henry Moore, Henri Matisse (1869–1954), Graham Sutherland and André Derain (1880–1954), undertaking multiple experiments to faithfully translate these works into screen-printed textiles.

FIG 53. The Aschers exploited the relatively new medium of screen-printing to faithfully translate artist's mark-making into the finished textile product. Henry Spencer Moore for Ascher (London) Ltd, *Three Standing Figures*, 'Artist's Square', *c*.1946. Screen-printed rayon. National Museums Scotland (K.2019.95), presented by the Art Fund.

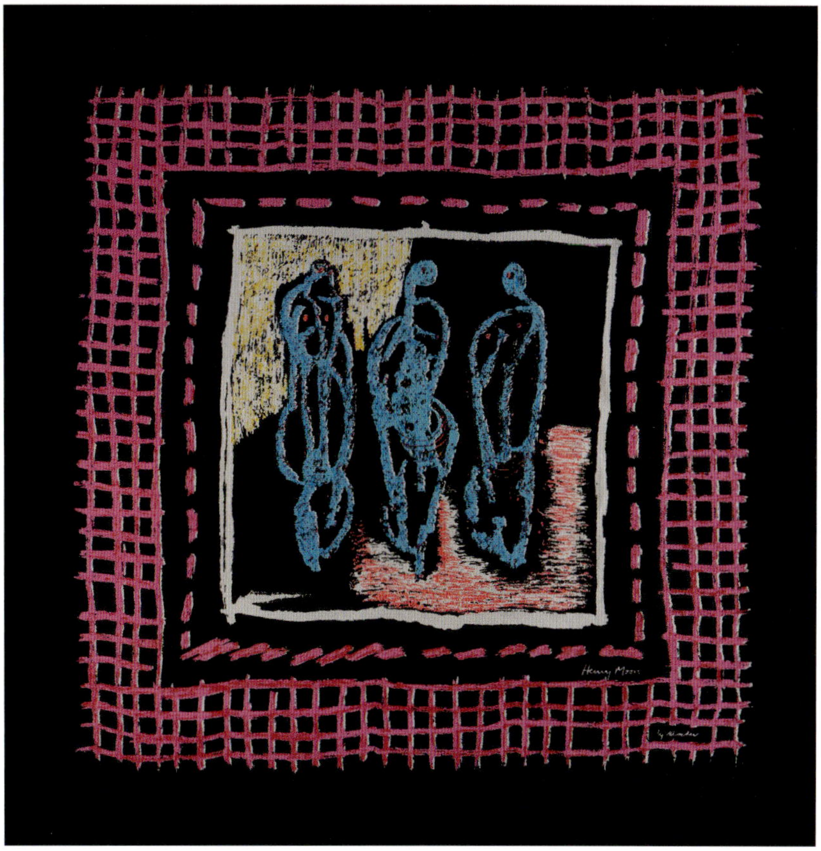

The Aschers' move to Britain was part of a wider pattern of migration: from the 1930s, the country saw an influx of creative practitioners seeking refuge from the spread of fascism across continental Europe. The émigré contribution to British fashion and visual culture has been the subject of recent publications and exhibitions, including *Fashion City: How Jewish Londoners Shaped Global Style*, staged at the Museum of London in 2023. Indeed, in the exhibition catalogue's foreword, the acclaimed fashion designer David Sassoon (1932–2025) states:

> I became aware of the Jewish involvement in the London fashion industry when I started working and met agents of the leading luxury fashion fabric companies, and lace and embroidery houses that we used. Many of the designer-owners with whom I dealt were Jewish, heading internationally important companies, including Zika Ascher of Ascher, famous for sumptuous silk prints, Bernat Klein, renowned for his ribbon-threaded silk tweed, and Miki Sekers of Sekers and The West Cumberland Silk Mills.[39]

FIG 54. Horrockses Fashions' advertisement featuring Sekers Fabrics, late 1950s. The Harris (2011.122).

FIG 55. OPPOSITE: Cocktail dress in a Sekers' nylon, transfer printed with a design of roses, Horrockses Fashions, late 1950s. The Harris (2001.35).

Many émigré designers had received progressive training in Central Europe (at institutions such as the Wiener Werkstätte, Reimann Schule and the Bauhaus) and brought exciting new visual languages and approaches to the UK during a time of change and reconstruction. These individuals had knowledge and skills relating to textile manufacture and garment production, having operated successful enterprises in their native countries, in addition to language skills and an international outlook, enabling them to operate successfully in an increasingly globalised industry.[40]

Horrockses Fashions benefited directly from émigré design and manufacturing talent, sourcing silks and synthetic fabrics from Sekers (West Cumberland Silk Mills), including high-quality satins and gauzes (54, 55).[41] The company was founded in 1938 by Hungarian émigré textile designer and manufacturer Nicholas 'Miki' Sekers in Whitehaven, Cumbria. Sekers was established with assistance from the Special Areas Legislation, initiated by the UK government in 1934, which financed factories in designated areas experiencing economic hardship.[42] Described by Anna Nyburg as 'a marriage made in heaven', this scheme brought refugee industrialists to the depressed north-east and north-west of England, creating hundreds of thousands of jobs.[43] Miki Sekers studied textile technology at Krefeld College in Germany and worked in his family's silk mill in Budapest before relocating to the UK. His company made the transition to producing synthetic parachute silk during wartime and began supplying textiles to couture houses including Molyneux, Dior and Givenchy.[44]

From its roots in the industrial expansion of north-west England in the late eighteenth century, Horrockses Fashions evolved to produce high-quality ready-to-wear garments for an increasingly affluent middle-class market. The garments themselves were skilfully adapted from Paris fashions for mass production, and the company's exclusive textiles set it apart from its contemporaries. Horrockses adopted a pluralistic approach to sourcing fresh new textile designs, and this is reflected in the sheer variety of the company's output. In museum collections and on the vintage market, the designs run the gamut from revivalism to abstract modernism. Wider educational and government initiatives and émigré practitioners were key to the company's success in keeping a steady stream of new ideas flowing into the company. At the heart of Horrockses Fashions was a network of individuals committed to making progressive design available to a mass market.

4 HORROCKSES FASHIONS Design Books Archive

SCOTT SCHIAVONE

Among the most significant archival holdings relating to Horrockses Fashions at The Harris are the design books originating from the office of the company's head designer, John Tullis. Acquired by the museum in 2011, these remarkable volumes provide an unparalleled insight into the creative and technical processes behind one of Britain's most successful mid-century fashion labels.

Nine design books survive in the collection. Each page presents a carefully composed record of a garment: an original pencil sketch of the design, a mounted swatch of the exact fabric used in production and a contemporary publicity photograph showing the completed dress worn by a model. Together, these elements document the transformation of an idea from sketch to finished garment, offering rare evidence of how Horrockses translated studio design into commercially successful fashion.

These books are invaluable tools as the combination of sketches, textiles and photography allows garments within the museum's collection to be dated with precision. This publication marks the first time material from the Horrockses' design books has been reproduced in print, making an important archival resource accessible to a wider audience.

A.166
PHOTOS BY
ROY ROUND

229

1901
659

1506

1607

503

49

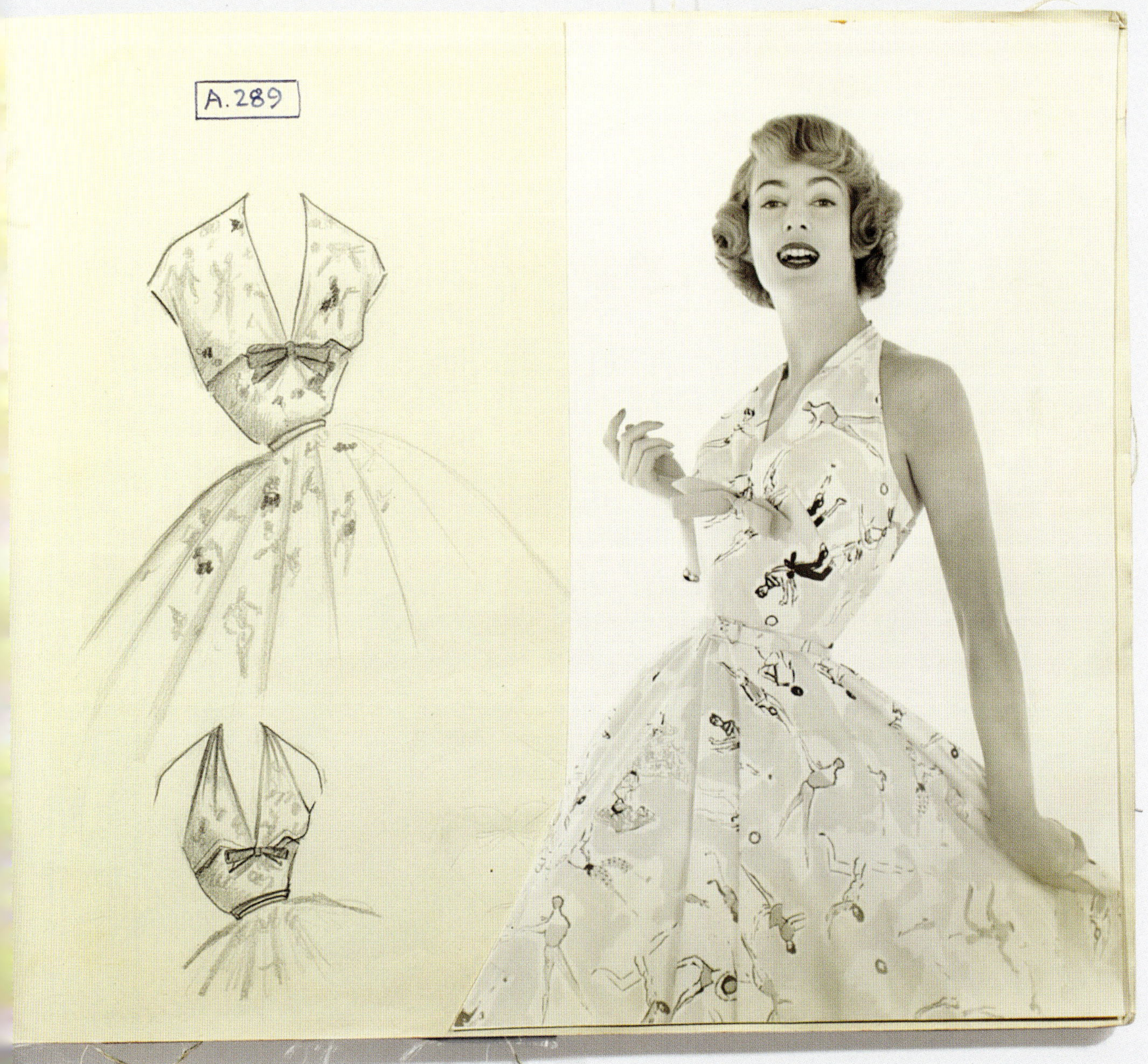
A.289

1531

1622

FIG 56. P. 73: Design for a floral housecoat. Horrockses Fashions design book, 1954. The Harris (2011.111.6_10).

FIG 57. PP. 74–75: Design for a sunsuit with lobster wrap skirt. Horrockses Fashions design book, 1954. Textile design by Pat Albeck. The Harris (2011.111.3_37).

FIG 58. PP. 76–77: Design for a day dress with chicken print and white piqué cotton bolero. Horrockses Fashions design book, 1954. The Harris (2011.111.8_01).

FIG 59. PP. 78–79: Design for a day dress. Horrockses Fashions design book, 1954. The Harris (2011.111.5_05).

FIG 60. PP. 80–81: Design for a cocktail dress and jacket. Horrockses Fashions design book, 1954. The Harris (2011.111.5_30).

FIG 61. PP. 82–83: Design for a bodice, crop trousers and penguin skirt. Horrockses Fashions design book, 1954. The Harris (2011.111.3_24).

FIG 62. PP. 84–85: Design for a cocktail dress and bolero with *tromp l'oeil* lace. Horrockses Fashions design book, 1954. The Harris (2011.111.4_15).

FIG 63. PP. 86–87: Design for a rose-print day dress with matching wrap. Horrockses Fashions design books, 1954. The Harris (2011.111.2_11).

FIG 64. PP. 88–89: Design for a summer dress with matching bolero. Horrockses Fashions design book, 1954. Textile design by Pat Albeck. The Harris (2011.111.6_30).

FIG 65. PP. 90–91: Design for a floral cocktail dress and pink corded jacket with matching floral lining. Horrockses Fashions design book, 1954. The Harris (2011.111. 5_14).

FIG 66. PP. 92–93: Design for a cocktail dress with black cummerbund sash and matching jacket. Horrockses Fashions design book, 1954. The Harris (2011.111.5_34).

FIG 67. OPPOSITE: Fabric swatch for a cocktail dress. Horrockses Fashions design book, 1953. The Harris (2011.111.1_02).

Horrockses Fashions
REGD.
in Fine Cotton
Hilmar

5 HORROCKSES FASHIONS AND THE LEGACY OF FLORAL FEMININITY

PAIGE BLAKE

Horrockses Fashions became one of the most distinctive and iconic British dress brands of the post-war era, celebrated for its vivid florals and the quintessential 1950s silhouette that reconnected women with a sense of femininity after years defined by conflict and austerity. In the pages of *Vogue*, a Horrockses' advertisement is almost impossible to overlook. Amid spreads dominated by wool, utility wear and military-inspired tailoring (68), the sudden appearance of bold colours, painterly florals and optimistic patterns feels almost like encountering technicolour after years of grey. These dresses did not simply decorate the page – they burst from it, embodying life, hope and post-war renewal (69).

While the brand experimented with a variety of motifs, florals became its signature. Historically, florals have symbolised femininity and Horrockses utilised this visual language. Yet its prints were not merely decorative; they also projected optimism and colour onto women's fashion, representing growth, life and softness after the war.

The Horrockses' silhouette itself – soft, full, elegant and unmistakably shaped by Christian Dior's (1905–1957) revolutionary 'New Look' – offered a dramatic contrast to the structured,

FIG 68. Advertisement for Horrockses Fashions in *Vogue*, 1949.

FIG 69. Sumrie advertisement, *c*.1940s.

pared-back lines of earlier wartime styles. With cinched waists and voluminous skirts, the 1950s silhouette became a visual for femininity across Europe, reclaiming luxury and abundance, consciously (or not) echoing Victorian ideals that framed the female body as overtly feminine. Horrockses embraced this silhouette in a less exaggerated version that balanced elegance with practicality. Its dresses were wearable, youthful and predominantly produced in washable cottons, yet they still carried the grandeur of Dior's vision (70).

The legacy of Horrockses' dresses is rich, inspiring and complex. Contemporary fashion continues to return to the aesthetic codes that Horrockses embodied – florals, soft shapes and nostalgic femininity – but these motifs now operate within a very different cultural landscape. Mid-century fashion often positioned florals and the hourglass silhouette as tools of idealisation; today, they could serve as instruments of self-expression, empowerment or patriarchal imposition. Looking back at Horrockses' garments through this contemporary lens enables us to appreciate the beauty and craftsmanship of their designs while also recognising the complexities they carried – how they offered joy and optimism, yet simultaneously reinforced narrow ideals of women. In reflecting on their influence, we can understand post-war femininity not as static, but as part of a longer continuum in which fashion negotiates the boundaries between expression, expectation and identity.

The Horrockses' iconic silhouette is based on Christian Dior's 1947 'New Look', which encapsulated femininity by exaggerating the traditional hourglass shape to celebrate what Dior termed 'ultra-femininity'.[1] This was heavily inspired by women's fashions in the Victorian era (1837–1901).[2] Their cinched waists and voluminous skirts were typically created by hooped underskirts and corsets. This silhouette functioned as a symbol of femininity and status, transforming women into a kind of walking spectacle. The connection to florals was undeniable: the skirt represented the bloom of a flower, while the corseted torso acted as the stem. Flowers and the Victorian era were deeply intertwined, with floriography being hugely popular; specific flowers were worn to express traits or emotions.[3] This symbolism entered women's fashion, where florals became tied to femininity through the *femme-fleur* (flower-woman), reinforcing the notion that women were beautiful, delicate and decorative – much like flowers.

FIG 70. Evening dress by Christian Dior, Paris, 1953.

Horrockses mirrored this silhouette in a softer, more practical form, then pushed the floral connection further by using floral prints and motifs.

The 1920s saw a dramatic shift in fashions. An androgynous silhouette emerged in *Vogue*'s fashion illustrations, and Gabrielle Chanel (1883–1971) pioneered the 'New Woman', marking a backlash against traditional femininity. This 'boyish' style was liberating compared to the restrictive corsetry of the previous century. Chanel could be viewed as a radical designer, with the Chanel look being described as a 'youthful, slender, boyish figure ... comfortable clothes and short hemlines', due to the loose fit, lack of corsetry and emphasis on the natural female form (71). She famously 'liberated the body, ... eliminated the waistline

FIG 71. Paris fashions by Chanel, 1923. Fashion illustration.

FIG 72. OPPOSITE: Cotton dressing gown with two-tone pink floral motif, Horrockses Fashions, *c.*1952–53. The Harris (2009.206).

and created a new silhouette'.[4] However, even these designs retained aspects of femininity through the use of materials and embellishments such as silks, satins, embroidery, beading and floral appliqués.

The 1950s arguably represent one of the most overtly feminine phases in modern fashion history, with taglines such as 'soft, charming and feminine' dominating advertising.[5] Dior's debut collection featured 'rounded shoulders, a cinched waist and a very full skirt',[6] creating a striking silhouette that quickly became synonymous with mid-century fashion. Dior's mission was to make 'women look like women again'.[7] Importantly, his first collection was named 'Corolle' after a botanical term referring to the part of a flower that opens into petals – with 'rounded shoulders' acting as the petals and the skirt representing the full blossom.[8] This parallel signals the designer's notion of the deep connection between femininity and nature. The *femme-fleur* ideal suggests that being female is inherently tied to appearing natural and decorative, closely linking back to the Victorian era.

Yet Dior's 'New Look' was not universally embraced. For some women it offered a welcome return to luxury, romanticism and femininity after years of war. The extravagance of Dior's designs contrasted sharply with wartime austerity and presented escapism through beauty and fashion. This feeling was articulated by Mrs Knowles, who owned a luxurious Horrockses Fashions' housecoat, now in the collection at The Harris, featuring a white cotton base and a printed floral motif in two-tone pink (72). Mrs Knowles wore it when she was in her late teens/early 20s, in the late 1940s/early 1950s. She remembered 'feeling very glamorous wearing this long dressing gown at home, particularly when she walked elegantly down the stairs with it trailing behind her'.[9] Experiences like this illustrate the significant emotional impact of clothing in the aftermath of hardship.

For others, however, the silhouette was 'repressive, conservative'.[10] Yet this silhouette became the defining style of the 1950s, dominating fashion and being worn by many women. Despite these mixed reactions, the influence of Dior's 'New Look' was profound and far-reaching. It shaped fashion trends across the Western world, including in Britain, where brands such as Horrockses Fashions incorporated elements of the style into its own designs. Horrockses allowed women to participate in this vision of femininity through lightweight cottons, cheerful prints

and more affordable pricing, offering an everyday alternative to couture. Yet even in these practical forms, the silhouette and floral motifs retained their symbolic significance, continuing to promote the image of women as flowers and reinforcing the *femme-fleur* ideal. Caroline Elenowitz-Hess suggests that the 'use of floral motifs in conjunction with modernist fashions, signalled a desire to draw upon and reinterpret these long-held signals of femininity, allowing for a new understanding of womanhood while evoking the familiar, eternal and procreative elements of flowers'.[11]

The ongoing popularity of flowers is more than due to the multitude of different examples. They are appealing because they are natural forms – beautiful, relevant and a source of inspiration. Flowers' allure may derive from the symmetry and patterns found in their leaves and petals. We may also admire flowers because they are transitory. Fleeting and fragile, their symbolic nature further reinforces why they have found their way onto textiles. Although flowers show up more prominently in certain decades, they remain a constant motif throughout fashion.[12]

Fashion historian Amy de la Haye notes that the rose has, for centuries, symbolised an idealised womanhood, making it one of the most persistent motifs used to represent femininity in dress. Victorian flower language made roses more than decoration: they became coded expressions of female character, morality and desire. This symbolic weight was carried forward into the twentieth century. De la Haye highlights that floral dress cannot be understood purely aesthetically; flowers act as emotional and political symbols, shaping and reflecting ideals of femininity.[13]

Although florals have been used in fashion for centuries, Horrockses' prints were particularly eye-catching because they were exclusive. The brand worked with a wide range of artists and designers, including Eduardo Paolozzi (1924–2005), Alastair Morton (1910–1963), Patricia 'Pat' Albeck (1930–2017), Joyce Badrocke (1926–2020) and Betty Newmarch (1921–2004).[14] The fact that some of them were women was significant at the time, because after the war women were encouraged to return to domestic roles. Horrockses provided creative, skilled employment and professional opportunities at a moment when these were limited for women. Although fashion has long been framed as 'women's work', particularly in relation to garment-making – with 'women across many cultures hav[ing] historically done much of the … sewing … in their communities for centuries' –

FIG 73. Horrockses' pattern book, 1950s. Lancashire Archives (DDX 2/34).

their participation in professional design roles still marked a shift forward in women's rights.[15]

Horrockses' choice to use mainly cotton was also notably progressive. The breathability and durability of cotton made its dresses genuinely wearable, giving women far more freedom to move. Unlike restrictive hoops and corsetry, these designs enabled women to be active rather than decorative. The prints themselves played a crucial role in shaping the brand's identity. Its florals were playful and embodied an idealised femininity that became especially desirable after years of more utilitarian, masculine wartime clothing. Its dresses were attractive to a broad age range, giving the brand a universal appeal.

Part of the enduring attraction of Horrockses' florals lies in their extraordinary variety. As evidenced in the Horrockses' pattern swatch books in the Lancashire Archives (73, 74, 75), there are hundreds of floral designs, all differing in colour, scale and artistic approach. This variety ensured that Horrockses' collections remained fresh. It is unsurprising that the brand is still adored today despite no longer actively operating – florals have timeless appeal and never go out of fashion.

Even when focusing solely on Horrockses' florals, the range was remarkably varied. Some designs were soft and romantic; others bold, strong or geometric. Throughout, femininity remained central, seen in the frequent use of pinks and delicate motifs that aligned

FIG 74. Horrockses' pattern book, 1950s. Lancashire Archives (DDX 2/34).

with the heightened ultra-femininity of the 1950s. This breadth meant there was a Horrockses' floral to suit every taste. One of the most recognisable motifs was the repeated floral stripe known as the 'floral bayadère stripe',[16] which encapsulated the brand's aesthetic.

Many Horrockses' prints incorporated roses. In *The Rose in Fashion*, the rose is described as carrying a duality – beautiful yet thorned – which reflects both the appeal and the complexity of femininity. When worn in fashion, roses are 'flowers that are [meant to be] looked at',[17] ensuring that those who see the dresses cannot help but be captivated, ultimately enhancing the desirability of the wearer and the garment alike. A Horrockses' pink dress is the epitome of femininity (76), the roses evoking innocence, love and devotion. The natural, soft colours connect to romanticism. The only contrast is provided by the stained-glass window effect of the stemmed roses, which are encircled by rose garlands.

A similar dress (139), but mirrored in a sherbet yellow with dainty floral motifs, connects women to sweetness and candy-like associations. Here, the floral elements are much softer, in a grey tone and swirling design. The little bows at the bottom of the shoulder straps provide a small touch of femininity and emphasise the romantic delicacy of the dress.

Another dress features a particularly naturalistic floral pattern. The vibrant coral tones of the roses suggest sweetness and youth (77). The full skirt has pleating that creates volume and the cinched waist silhouette elevates this 1950s style. The bolero in the same fabric, a signature Horrockses' addition, provides an element of fun as well as modesty. The coral pink bow under the bust ties in with the colour of the roses. This dress was donated and worn by Mrs Webster, who purchased it 'especially for a dinner dance' in 1959, suggesting Horrockses' high reputation.[18]

Maryse Addison, a dedicated admirer and wearer of the Horrockses' brand, donated 23 Horrockses Fashions'-related objects to The Harris Museum in 2016 (24, 25). Two dresses stand out.

FIG 75. Horrockses' pattern and order sample design books, c.1900–51. Lancashire Archives (DDHS/29/10).

FIG 76. Cotton summer dresses with pink roses, Horrockses Fashions, *c.*1955. The Harris (2020.18).

FIG 77. Cotton cocktail dress and bolero with vibrant coral roses and green foliage, Horrockses Fashions, *c.*1956–59. The Harris (2000.298).

The first dress, a particularly beautiful and quintessentially feminine garment, boasts a palette of baby blue that automatically links to ideas of femininity, reinforced by the dainty embroidered white daisies. The deep V-neckline and the directional shift in the floral placement create contrast with the bayadère-striped skirt, while the ruched detailing at the waist further enhances the classic 1950s silhouette, giving the dress its elegant structure and gentle fullness.

The second dress is very feminine with a classic 1950s silhouette. It too has ruched fabric at the waist, although slightly less exaggerated in form, and has wide spaghetti straps and a square neckline. The muted purple background reinforces associations with femininity, while the daisies continue the *femme-fleur* theme.

While the boldness of the daisy motif in a pink Horrockses' day dress could be seen as a departure from traditional softness, the persistent use of daisy imagery maintains its link to femininity (80). Additionally, pastel pink is a highly gendered colour, which reinforces the era's ultra-femininity. The grey daisies contrast with the pink background and vary in scale, grasping the viewers' attention. The sweet bow at the base of the V-neckline evokes femininity and softness. The matching patterned belt enhances the classic 1950s silhouette further still. The daisy was a popular Horrockses' motif and has connotations of 'innocence, childhood and purity'.[19] The diversity of Horrockses' floral motifs showcased their versatility, while maintaining a cohesive brand identity firmly rooted in femininity.

The colour palette of Horrockses' dresses also played a significant role in embracing ultra-femininity. Pastel tones were used repeatedly, contributing to an aesthetic that was traditionally 'ladylike'. In magazines of the time, 'female models [were often presented] with a more traditionally feminine colour range of whiter and lighter shades, that promote a more "innocent" or "pure" form of femininity'.[20] This palette aligns with the broader cultural association of pastel colours with femininity. Pink, in particular, has long been regarded as a symbol of femininity in Western culture, and its frequent use by Horrockses emphasised this association, especially within its florals.[21]

In aligning women with nature – seen as delicate, decorative and nurturing – the floral motif perpetuated feminine ideologies.[22] By examining the patterns, motifs and colour palettes of

FIG 78. Cotton summer dress with white daisy pattern, Horrockses Fashions, *c.*1950s. The Harris (2016.12.12).

FIG 79. Blue cotton dress with white broderie anglaise overlayer, Horrockses Fashions, *c.*1956. The Harris (2016.12.14).

FIG 80. Pink cotton dress with grey daisies, Horrockses Fashions, *c.*1950s. The Harris (2022.7.3).

Horrockses' dresses, it becomes clear that its designs were more than just fabric and thread; they were cultural artefacts, deeply intertwined with the ideology and escapism of the 1950s.

Since then, femininity has fluctuated in fashion. The 1960s saw a rejection of hyper femininity (82), with designers such as Mary Quant (1930–2023) pioneering the emergence of the mini-skirt (83) in contrast to the demure ideal promoted by Dior and emulated by Horrockses. There was a shift from the tightly defined waist that had dominated women's fashion since 1947 to a more modern, controversial silhouette.[23]

Florals came back into fashion with Laura Ashley, which in the 1970s and 1980s was renowned for its 'floral chintz fashions'[24] and 'flowing flowery frocks'[25] inspired by Victorian florals.[26] The *femme-fleur* may have been placed on women's clothing during this period of political upheaval as a peaceful image providing comfort and recognisable values[27](81).

FIG 81. Laura Ashley clothing magazine advertisement, *c.*1980s.

With the shift and progression of social norms, women in general have worn more masculine clothing, probably due to a greater number of women being in work and requiring clothing that is practical, functional and professional rather than decorative.[28] However, although trends have come and gone, florals and femininity (whether ruffles, silhouette or fabric) have never been completely out of style.

Floral motifs, once derided as merely pretty or passive, can be argued to have had a resurgence in contemporary feminist visual culture. At women's marches and rallies, protesters wear wreaths and carry bouquets, and posters incorporate flowers entwined with slogans. Far from retreating into traditionalism, this 'floral feminism' reclaims femininity, signifying resilience and defiance: delicate petals become a symbol of empowerment. For example, in *Imágen de Yágul* (1973) (84) Ana Mendieta used wildflowers scattered over her nude body to turn an image of softness into one of strength and renewal, connecting to Mother Nature and disrupting the male gaze.[29] From this we can infer that the *femme-fleur* is not necessarily something that should be perceived as negative; it is also powerful and wonderful, which women have reclaimed and used to symbolise strength and beauty. Horrockses' influence can be seen to this day in dresses with similar silhouettes and floral patterns. Current trends such as cottagecore and tradwife take inspiration from the 1950s.[30] Increasing political uncertainty frequently coincides with a resurgence of romanticised femininity in fashion.

Horrockses' dresses are still much loved, by those who used to wear them, by vintage collectors and by those who have donated them to The Harris collection. Despite the trends, we may look back at the 1950s as deeply problematic and not necessarily to be admired, as they marked a highly restrictive and overtly sexist social climate for women. Post-war fashion often reinforced traditional gender roles, domestic confinement and a narrowing of female autonomy, representing in many ways a step backwards for women's rights rather than a progressive moment of liberation. Nevertheless, women have embraced the style and silhouettes of 1950s fashion and greatly appreciate its influence and heritage. Although these revived styles are inseparable from the social contexts of their origin, women today have reclaimed them to align with their present-day ideals.[31]

Ultimately, though, the meaning of floral femininity remains contested: are petals and flowers demonstrating defiance or

FIG 82. Cream wool dress and cape, Mary Quant's Ginger Group, *c.*1966–68. The Harris (1988.11).

submission/compliance? While floral prints are often linked to ideas of softness and femininity, they have also been reappropriated repeatedly in fashion as a means of feminist empowerment.[32] Through fashion's influence – whether its silhouettes or florals – femininity is reinforced. Fashion can restrict and empower women simultaneously.[33] This sentiment is particularly evident in the influence of 1950s Horrockses Fashions, making these dresses beautiful but equally complicated and complicit.

In recent years, the influence of Horrockses' florals and silhouettes can be seen in the collections of contemporary brands whose romantic, cinched-waist dresses echo the optimism and fcmininity of thc 1950s. Thc cottagccorc trcnd, populariscd on social media, similarly draws on nostalgic motifs of florals and soft shapes, offering a modern reinterpretation of post-war ideals. At the same time, floral prints have become symbols of empowerment in feminist movements, with protestors using flower crowns and motifs to signal resilience and solidarity. Fashion exhibitions continue to celebrate the legacy of brands

FIG 83. Campaign to Support the Mini-Skirt, London, 1966.

FIG 84. *Imágen de Yágul*, 1973. Ana Mendieta.

FIG 85. OPPOSITE: Cotton dress in navy with white roses and green foliage, Horrockses Fashions, *c.*1958. The Harris (2025.8).

like Horrockses, highlighting their enduring appeal and the evolving meanings of femininity in dress. These contemporary perspectives show that while the language of florals and femininity is rooted in history, it remains dynamic and contested in today's cultural landscape.

Emerging as a distinctive British brand in the aftermath of the war, Horrockses' bright, cheerful dresses offered welcome relief from years of austerity. The vivid prints felt optimistic, marking a return to colour, comfort and everyday femininity. Yet, looking back, the influence of Dior's 'New Look' silhouette casts a shadow. While Horrockses' softer shapes and practical cotton fabrics made its styles far more wearable and less ornamental than couture, they still drew from the same foundations.

Horrockses reveals how fashion both reflects and reinforces its cultural moment. Its florals – roses, daisies and countless playful prints – appear light-hearted on the surface, but they participated in a wider post-war return to the feminine ideal. They echoed the era's expectations of womanhood, however gently, situating women back within a restrictive model.

And yet, Horrockses' garments were also beloved. They were bought, worn and cherished by women who found joy in their colours and freedom in their movement. This tension is what defines their legacy. The dresses feel innocent and uplifting, but they also carry traces of the political and cultural ideals that shaped them. Later feminist movements may reinterpret florals as symbols of strength or protest, but Horrockses' foundations remain tied to a mid-century vision of femininity – one that still echoes through contemporary floral fashion.

To look back at Horrockses, then, is to hold both truths at once: the beauty of the dresses, their craft and their cultural impact; and the weight of the ideals they quietly upheld. Their influence endures, but so do the shadows of the era that produced them. In this way, Horrockses Fashions reminds us that floral prints and feminine silhouettes are never merely decorative – they are part of a longer lineage of meaning, one that continues to shape how femininity is imagined, expressed and expected in fashion today.

6 HORROCKSES FASHIONS AND ROYAL STYLE

MATTHEW STOREY

Members of the British royal family wore and promoted Horrockses Fashions at the height of the company's success in the 1950s. Horrockses was perfect for the strategy of royal image-making through clothing, communicating the values of its royal wearers through widely seen photographs and media reports.

As a British-made fashion brand, wearing Horrockses was a way of visibly supporting British manufacture, part of a long tradition in royal fashion patronage. As early as the eighteenth century, Queen Caroline (1683–1737), Princess Augusta (1719–1772) and Queen Charlotte (1744–1818) all promoted wearing British-made textiles.[1] Queen Victoria (1819–1901) is credited with reviving the Honiton lace industry in Devon by choosing it for her wedding in 1840 (88). She wore the lace throughout her reign as a key component of her image-making, and insisted other members of her family patronised the industry.[2] While Queen Alexandra (1844–1925) was notable for her use of Parisian as well as British fashion houses, she was in many ways the exception (87). The trend for royal women, and particularly those closest to the line of succession, to wear British fashion was deliberately followed in the twentieth century and continues today.

FIG 86. The Queen's Sunshine Wardrobe. *Picture Post*, 8 February 1954, p. 24.

FIG 87. Queen Alexandra pictured in later life wearing a magnificent toque style hat, *c.*1910.

FIG 88. Queen Victoria wearing a gown of Honiton lace, 1854. Photographed by Roger Fenton.

In their public wardrobes in the first half of the twentieth century this was most visibly manifested in clothing made by leading elite dressmakers and couturiers. Queen Mary (1867–1953) patronised Reville & Rossiter and Queen Elizabeth The Queen Mother (1900–2002) favoured Madame Handley-Seymour (1867–1948) and then Norman Hartnell (1901–1979). Queen Elizabeth II (1926–2022) turned to Hartnell, and then Hardy Amies (1909–2003) for her most important clothes. All placed royal dressing in the realm of clothing accessible only to the wealthiest women in society, with a formality appropriate to their station. However, the 1940s and 1950s also saw a general relaxation and modernisation of royal and court dress codes. Although the first decades of the twentieth century had seen a strict regulation of court dress, with rules published with the authority of the Lord Chamberlain in successive editions of *Dress and Insignia Worn at His Majesty's Court*, the final edition was published in 1937 and was not subsequently updated. While women had been expected to attend court presentations in mandatory evening dress, trains and feather plumes, after the Second World War these events moved to the daytime, with day dresses worn, before the custom was abolished by Elizabeth II in 1958.

The exclusivity and unattainability of clothing worn by members of the royal family were tempered by a desire to design a look that was approachable. Hartnell's use of soft pastel colours for Queen Elizabeth The Queen Mother, with hats with brims that revealed her face, created a comforting and relatable style. The power of this image-making was particularly important for her widely publicised and popular visits to bombed areas of the country during the war. Her decision to dress her daughters in matching Liberty cotton print dresses in the 1930s was a precedent

FIG 89. Liberty print floral cotton dresses worn by Queen Elizabeth II and Princess Margaret, 1936. Royal Ceremonial Dress Collection, Historic Royal Palaces.

FIG 90. Queen Mary at Horrockses in 1948.

for the later adoption of Horrockses' garments (89). The simple but beautifully made cotton dresses, often identical, presented not only an image of equality between the siblings, but also of relatable domesticity. Pictured in the kind of cotton dresses that many of the public could have worn, frequently alongside their parents, the styling of Princesses Elizabeth and Margaret (1930–2002) presented a familial image of monarchy at a time of upheaval for the royal family after the abdication of the Duke of Windsor (1894–1972), and of international instability in the lead up to the war.

There had been a history of royal engagement with Horrockses long before the launch of the Horrockses Fashions brand in 1946. Queen Mary and George V (1865–1936) had visited the Horrockses' mill as part of a trip to Preston in 1913, where their cars passed underneath an arch made of bales of cotton as cheering crowds looked on.[3] Queen Mary went to the St George Street offices of Horrockses Fashions on Hanover Square in 1948, where she was photographed inspecting the cotton of a dress worn by a model (90). The quality of the material was probably of more interest to the Queen, who was then in her early 80s and fully established in her conservative dress sense, than the youthful styling of the dress itself. Instead, younger and more fashionable members of the family began to wear the brand, including Princess Margaret, Princess Alice, Duchess of Gloucester (1901–2004), Princess Mary, Countess of Harewood (1897–1965), Princess Marina, Duchess of Kent (91) (1906–1968), and Princess Alexandra (b. 1936).[4]

The choice by Queen Elizabeth II to wear Horrockses Fashions gave the most visible royal support to the brand. The young Queen's accession in 1952 and coronation in 1953 provided a much-needed feeling of renewal and optimism for a public still affected by austerity and the aftermath of war. The coronation was enthusiastically celebrated, with British designers and manufacturers

FIG 91. Princess Marina, Duchess of Kent, wearing a Horrockses' ensemble in May 1953.

FIG 92. Detail of the Coronation commemoration dress in taupe, designed by Margaret Meades, Horrockses Fashions, 1953. The Harris (2004.11).

FIG 93. OPPOSITE: Coronation commemoration dress, designed by Margaret Meades in 1953 (with modern belt). Royal Ceremonial Dress Collection, Historic Royal Palaces.

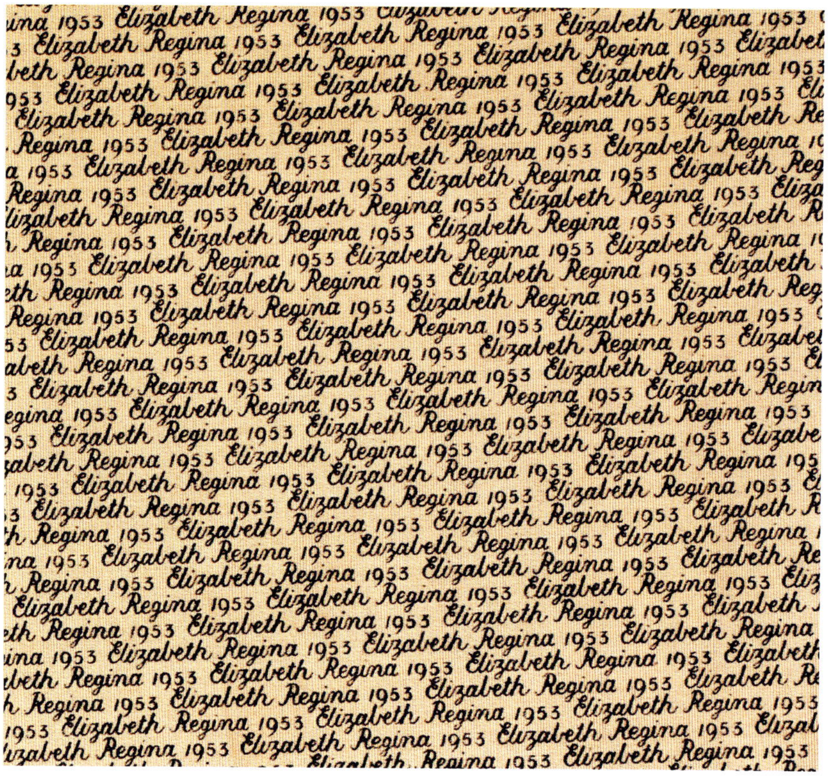

producing vast amounts of commemorative merchandise. Margaret Meades (1925–2014) designed one of Horrockses' most distinctive and unusual designs to mark the event, a printed cotton with the small repeated text 'Elizabeth Regina 1953' in black letters on several different background colourways (92, 93). The coronation had filled magazines and newsreels, and the international attention on the newly crowned Queen continued with her six-month tour of the Commonwealth, beginning in November 1953, during which she wore Horrockses' designs.

Queen Elizabeth's wardrobe for the tour was widely reported on. Norman Hartnell and Hardy Amies provided many of the Queen's afternoon and evening dresses, with Hartnell saying, 'I wanted to capture the sunshine and blue skies of the countries she was to visit'.[5] The two couturiers' creations were admired, but were unique and unobtainable by readers of the many articles devoted to the clothes worn on the tour. However, press coverage repeatedly emphasised the accessibility of the Horrockses' day dress designs. *Picture Post*, in its February 1954 feature 'Sunshine clothes for sunny lands', noted that the 'off-the-peg' version of an attractive yellow floral dress was 'available in many shops, priced at £4 19s. 6d.' (86, 94).[6] This coverage extended to the press

in the countries visited on the tour. The Australian *Daily Telegraph Women's Magazine* entreated readers to 'Copy Her Majesty ... her dresses are here'. The Horrockses' dresses would be available in 'the same colours, designs, and fabrics as the Queen chose', but crucially would 'not be allowed for sale until after she had left Australia'.[7]

Horrockses carefully maintained this dual messaging of accessibility and exclusivity when dressing Queen Elizabeth II and other members of the royal family. The Queen's Horrockses' dresses were based on ready-to-wear designs, but custom-made to fit her. They were also not available for the public to buy until after she had worn them, further preserving the exclusivity expected when dressing royalty. The *Daily Telegraph* may have claimed that 'the Queen does not mind seeing the same dress on someone else' in relation to her official visit to Nigeria in 1955, but this was only on the strict condition that the designs were not released by Horrockses until after her departure from the country.[8] Horrockses was prepared to defend this, and successfully sued the *Daily Sketch* for wrongly reporting that they had sold

FIG 94. The Queen's Sunshine Wardrobe. *Picture Post*, 8 February 1954, p. 24.

FIG 95. Queen Elizabeth II wearing a later Horrockses' dress during her visit to Tuvalu in 1982.

designs supplied to the Queen before she had worn them.[9] This strategy allowed the royal wearer to retain some of the advantages of couture creations, while enjoying the benefits of appearing more relatable and democratic by choosing ready-to-wear.

Wearing Horrockses alongside couture on highly publicised overseas visits allowed members of the royal family to engage with two distinct aspects of design and society in 1950s Britain. If the 1953 coronation had represented a moment of national cohesiveness and renewal through tradition, ceremony and the display of ancient and aristocratic power, the 1951 Festival of Britain had showcased modernist design and a socialist future defined by a new welfare state.[10] In this context, the repeated emphasis in the press on the ability of the public to be able to wear identical Horrockses' designs to those worn by members of the royal family on overseas tours, while highlighting their affordable price, presented a strongly democratic picture. This was expressed in parallel to descriptions of bespoke couture creations, often carefully designed to make diplomatic reference to the symbols of host nations. The combination of modernity and tradition was a powerful and useful narrative for the royal family during a time of post-war change for the UK and the Commonwealth (95).

The blending of accessibility and exclusivity was inherent to the Horrockses' brand, making the supply of clothing to the royal family mutually beneficial. The St George Street offices and showroom placed Horrockses at the heart of London's elite clothing industry. 'Specials' could be created on-site for select women introduced to the company, including royalty. This allowed for designs to be slightly altered, and made after several fittings, in a method close to couture fashion.[11] Despite this, the majority of Horrockses' garments could be bought by better-off middle-class women, or others who felt that saving up for a well-designed, good-quality garment was worth the effort.[12] The use of fine artists to design textiles established the brand within a larger cultural conversation, and it is no surprise that a modernist design by Louis le Brocquy (1916–2012) appealed to the culturally engaged Princess Margaret for her 1956 tour of Africa (97).[13]

The Royal Ceremonial Dress Collection, cared for by Historic Royal Palaces, holds a later Horrockses Fashions'

FIG 96. Princess Margaret with Lord Snowdon in Nassau in the Bahamas in 1967.

FIG 97. Princess Margaret at a game farm in Tanganyika during her royal tour of East Africa in 1956.

FIG 98. Princess Margaret's Horrockses Fashions' printed cotton summer dress and matching bodice, 1967.

dress worn by Princess Margaret. It was made after the 1964 sale of the brand to Steinberg & Sons. She wore the short sundress, with a separate matching bodice, on holiday at Nassau in the Bahamas in March 1967 (96, 98). The press commented on the Princess's casual holiday styling, with the *Sunday Mirror* captioning a front-page photograph of her and Lord Snowdon: 'The royal art of taking things easy'.[14] At this time, the royal couple were seen as fashion and cultural leaders, and the Princess's styling of the dress with flat shoes and a large pair of gold and pearl earrings created a look that was both elevated and informal. Despite the strains that had begun to appear in their relationship, one photographer at the scene apparently commented of the couple: 'They were perfect – and obviously happy to be together'.[15] The dress is a key example of the power of a well-chosen Horrockses Fashions' outfit in successful royal image-making.

7 COUTURE CONNECTIONS
From Preston to Paris via London

SCOTT SCHIAVONE

FIG 99. Red velvet and satin cocktail dress, Horrockses Fashions, *c*.1956. The Harris (2016.12.1).

Launched in 1946, at a time when clothing rationing was still in place, Horrockses Fashions quickly positioned itself as one of Britain's leading ready-to-wear brands. Its mission was clear: to elevate ready-to-wear and reposition it as an industry associated with refinement and glamour. Central to this vision was a deliberate and sustained engagement with the aesthetics and prestige of Parisian haute couture.

In the years following the Second World War, Paris reaffirmed itself as the undisputed capital of fashion. Epitomised by the launch of Christian Dior's 'New Look' in 1947, this new silhouette, defined by cinched waists, sloping shoulders and voluminous skirts, rejected wartime austerity in favour of opulence and romantic femininity. The impact on European fashion was immediate and profound.

This chapter explores how Horrockses Fashions navigated the complex terrain between couture aspiration and ready-to-wear reality. Through close analysis of garments, promotional imagery and internal company records, it traces the brand's pursuit of exclusivity, its flirtation with couture methods and the tension between high style and industrial scalability. In doing so,

FIG 100. Horrockses' headquarters, 15 St George Street, Hanover Square, London. Lancashire Archives (DDX 2171/8).

it repositions Horrockses Fashions as a key player in the post-war reconfiguration of fashion hierarchy, when the codes of couture were appropriated, adapted and ultimately democratised.

15 St George Street, Hanover Square

In a strategic effort to distinguish itself from other British ready-to-wear brands, Horrockses Fashions established its headquarters at 15 St George Street, Hanover Square, London (100). Located in the heart of Mayfair, the epicentre of British couture, the address placed Horrockses in close proximity to the ateliers of leading couturiers such as Norman Hartnell (1901–1979), Victor Stiebel (1907–1976) and John Cavanagh (1914–2003). This deliberate positioning conferred upon the brand a sense of prestige by association.

Within 15 St George Street, Horrockses Fashions established its showrooms and design studio. Each season, in a manner reminiscent of the couture calendar, the company unveiled its new collections through exclusive presentations attended by prominent society figures and celebrities, including Queen Mary (1867–1953) and Clementine Churchill (1885–1977; wife of Winston Churchill) (101). These fashion shows elevated the status of the garments beyond mass-produced fashion, positioning them instead within the sphere of cultivated taste and discernment.

Echoing the architectural language of the couture salons of Paris, the interiors of the headquarters were designed with this in mind. Fresh floral arrangements adorned the entrance, framing a grand staircase that led to an elegant first-floor salon. The space, with its eighteenth-century proportions, conjured the opulence and intimacy of a couture presentation, ensuring that the Horrockses' experience resonated with notions of luxury and sophistication (102).

FIG 101. Her Majesty Queen Mary visits Horrockses, England, UK, 1948. Victoria and Albert Museum, London.

FIG 102. Horrockses' headquarters, *c.*1950. Drawing by Henky Sikinger. Lancashire Archives (DDX 2900/6).

FIG 103. Fashion designer John Tullis at work in his studio office in London, December 1959.

John Tullis, 'our couturier'

In 1950 Horrockses Fashions appointed John Tullis (1920–2004) (103) as its principal designer, a strategic decision that underscored the brand's ambition to align its ready-to-wear collections with the aesthetics of haute couture. Tullis, then 28 years old and born in South Africa, brought with him a pedigree rooted in the world of high fashion. He had trained under his mother's cousin, the esteemed British-born Parisian couturier Edward Molyneux (1891–1974), and had gained further experience with the prominent London couturier Norman Hartnell.

Tullis's couture background was essential to his role at Horrockses, where he was tasked with designing the more exclusive, prestige garments within the collection. His presence introduced a new level of creative tension and aspiration among the in-house design team. Internal correspondence from 1951 reveals that 'since the appointment of Mr Tullis, an element of competition has crept in amongst the stylists and there is a noticeable tendency to produce the "model" type of garment which is unsuitable for semi-mass production.'[1] This statement both acknowledges the aspirational standard set by Tullis and points to the operational tensions that arose when couture aesthetics collided with the practicalities of ready-to-wear manufacture.

FIG 104. Buyers being shown Horrockses Fashions' products at 15 St George Street, 1950.

Despite the internal recognition of Tullis's influence, Horrockses Fashions maintained a strict policy of corporate authorship. Individual designers were not to be credited publicly for their work. When British *Vogue* referred to a wedding dress in its May 1951 issue as designed by 'John Tullis for Horrockses',[2] the company's Managing Director, Herbert Mallot, delivered a swift rebuke. In a letter dated 2 May 1951, he wrote:

> Horrockses fashion production is, in future, described as such and that no reference is made to the individual who created it [...] I would stress that the goodwill of our fashion business must remain in the name of Horrockses and not in the name of anyone who is employed by us.[3]

However, despite this carefully managed anonymity, Tullis's profile within the industry continued to rise. A striking example of this appeared in the *News Chronicle* on 18 May 1954, which referred to Tullis as 'our couturier'.[4] The article celebrated his unusual career

FIG 105. Eileen Joyce in a Horrockses Fashions' 'Special', *c.*1947–49.

trajectory: 'He left the rarefied atmosphere of High Fashion at the £100 level for the wholesale dress trade.'[5] Journalist Jean Soward drew attention to Tullis's ability to translate the codes of couture into accessible fashion, positioning him as a rare talent capable of bridging social and commercial divides. Her commentary on Horrockses' seasonal fashion premieres was especially telling: 'There is no other fashion premiere in London today so like a Paris premiere in atmosphere and interest [...] This in a nutshell is John Tullis.'[6]

This direct comparison between the presentations of Horrockses and the revered Parisian couture calendar speaks volumes. It affirms not only Tullis's personal influence but also the degree to which his presence helped elevate Horrockses Fashions into a position of prestige within the British fashion landscape.

Horrockses' 'Specials'

Within the operational framework of Horrockses Fashions, a category of garments known as 'Specials' occupied a unique and elevated status. These were select styles adapted from the main seasonal collections, produced for exclusive clients. Such clients typically included well-known actresses, members of the aristocracy and occasionally royalty – figures whose social prominence was regarded by the brand as strategically valuable.

The process of commissioning a 'Special' echoed the traditions of haute couture. Clients were afforded the luxury of two to three fittings and were permitted to request slight modifications to personalise the design (105, 106). While this practice allowed Horrockses Fashions to emulate the rituals and allure of couture production, it did so without fully adopting its logistical or artisanal complexity. In essence, 'Specials' offered an accessible form of semi-bespoke fashion within a ready-to-wear context, bridging mass production and individual exclusivity.

However, despite their promotional potential, the production of 'Specials' increasingly came into conflict with the company's core business model. As a volume-based ready-to-wear enterprise, Horrockses Fashions depended on the efficiency of its design-to-distribution model. Internal records from a board meeting held on 6 August 1951 reveal mounting concern. James Cleveland Belle (1910–1983), the Design Director, acknowledged that the creation of 'Specials' had significantly disrupted the company's production calendar, remarking: 'for the coming season a decision must be

FIG 106. Cotton wedding ensemble with pocket detail and trimmed broderie anglaise, Horrockses Fashions, *c.*1951. The Harris (2021.3.1).

taken to refuse to make specials [...] as the making of special garments [...] hindered last year's programme to a great extent'.[7]

A detailed sales analysis for the 1950–51 season, dated 27 May 1951, provides further insight.[8] Of the 153 styles featured in the first collection, only ten were evening dresses (six in cotton, four in jersey). The second collection comprised 116 styles, including 18 evening dresses evenly split between cotton and jersey. Of these, just three 'Specials' were produced per fabric category. While limited in quantity, these garments required disproportionate time and labour.

This disparity is underscored in a report written by Mr W. Kerr assessing the delays in fulfilling the Spring 1951 collection: 'Between March and June 1951, there were 98 specials delivered and 27 were still in work. This involved fitting and

FIG 107. The Bar suit, Christian Dior 1947 collection, modelled by Renée Breton in Paris, 1955.

dealing with 53 people.'[9] Because the cost and strain on internal resources were so substantial, Kerr concluded that the London sampling department, then responsible for both showroom samples and 'Specials', was being stretched beyond its limits.

To mitigate these tensions, Kerr recommended a structural reorganisation: the formation of a dedicated department to handle 'Specials' independently from the main sampling operations. He even proposed that this new division be run as a 'retail semi-couturière establishment',[10] an evocative phrase that reveals how closely Horrockses Fashions had aligned itself, both ideologically and operationally, with the codes and cachet of couture.

FIG 108. TOP: Yellow evening gown by Lanvin-Castillo, 1950s. Brighton Museum & Art Gallery (R6140/6).

FIG 109. BOTTOM: Cocktail dress by Jean Dessès, 1950s. Brighton Museum & Art Gallery (R6140/4).

Looking to Paris and London

Horrockses Fashions strategically aligned itself with the aesthetic authority of Parisian and London couture in order to position its ready-to-wear collections at the forefront of British design. During the late 1940s and early 1950s, a 'Golden Age' of haute couture ensued and the label of a Paris couturier conferred prestige, elegance and an unquestionable standard of taste.

The single defining moment of this era came on 12 February 1947. Christian Dior's (1905–1957) inaugural collection, later dubbed the 'New Look' by American *Harper's Bazaar* editor Carmel Snow, introduced a radical new silhouette that would reconfigure the visual lexicon of mid-century fashion (107).[11] Dior's vision created a widespread shift across the European fashion industry. Couture houses rapidly adapted their silhouettes to reflect the 'New Look', and the formula of sloping shoulders, narrowed waistlines and full skirts quickly became the dominant mode.

Ready-to-wear companies were equally influenced by Paris. At Horrockses, this was not incidental but deliberate and embedded into the company's design strategy. Belle explicitly encouraged his design team to see the Paris couture collections prior to finalising its seasonal ranges. In a planning meeting held on 27 July 1949, Belle underscored the significance of this engagement: 'It is very important that they should see the next French collection to be shown in Paris in February 1950.'[12] He later noted that Horrockses' forthcoming collections 'could include modifications suggested by the Paris Collections in February 1950 and any new styles that had been developed'.[13]

Horrockses Fashions made formal applications to the Board of Trade to obtain permits allowing it to purchase couture garments directly from Paris. These items would be studied in Horrockses' London design studio, enabling the design team to examine couture construction techniques and silhouette lines first hand.

The success of the brand's application for a Board of Trade permit is evidenced by the survival of two Paris couture garments in the collection at Brighton Museum. These dresses, one by Antonio Castillo (1908–1984) for Lanvin (108) and the other by Jean Dessès (1904–1970) (109), were part of the reference wardrobe held at the London design studio. Donated to the museum in 2016, the garments once belonged to Maryse Addison, whose brother Anthony served as a designer for Horrockses in London.

Their presence within the studio context illustrates the company's direct engagement with French couture, reinforcing the brand's commitment to distilling Parisian innovation into accessible British ready-to-wear design.

Studio couture: Dessès and Lanvin

The Lanvin-Castillo dress in buttercup-yellow chiffon and taffeta uses draping and pleating to define its silhouette. The fitted bodice with shaped seams gives way to a voluminous skirt supported by internal layers of netting, typical of the mid-century couture's emphasis on dramatic volume. The sweetheart neckline exudes softness and femininity, while the sweeping drapery imbues the garment with a sense of historicism typical of 1950s couture. The entire garment is underpinned by meticulous hand-finishing and a rigid interior structure to ensure precision in shape and fit (108).

The cocktail dress by Jean Dessès dates to around 1954–55 and is made from a dark blue and green silk chiffon. It is a sophisticated example of 1950s draping and sculptural bodice work. The construction of the bodice, with its pleated, wrap-like folds, demonstrates Dessès' classical training and deep engagement with Greco-Roman aesthetics. The diaphanous layering of fabric across the bust and hips accentuates the natural lines of the body while conveying a sense of softness and fluidity. Beneath the surface, however, lies a structure of internal corsetry and precise pattern-cutting that defines the highest level of couture craftsmanship (110).

A Horrockses Fashions' cotton evening dress (113) from the same period shares significant stylistic DNA with its couture counterparts. Its hourglass silhouette, asymmetrical shoulder strap and back bodice ruching all echo the designs of Dessès, while its dramatic drapery recalls the sweeping panels of Lanvin-Castillo. Both couture and Horrockses' examples show a refined technical handling of bulk and shaping, with details such as the carefully placed side zip and sculptural pleating demonstrating sophisticated fabric manipulation (111, 112, 113).

Together, these garments speak to a broader mid-century tendency to reinterpret historical silhouettes. The Lanvin-Castillo gown, with its tightly fitted bodice, voluminous floor-length skirt and ethereal layers of chiffon, evokes the romantic elegance of the nineteenth century, particularly the opulence of early haute couture pioneered by Charles Frederick Worth (1825–1895).

FIGS 110 AND 111. TOP AND CENTRE: Details of yellow evening gown by Lanvin-Castillo, around 1954–55. Brighton Museum & Art Gallery (R6140/6).

FIG 112. BOTTOM: Detail of cocktail dress by Jean Dessès, around 1954–55. Brighton Museum & Art Gallery (R6140/4).

FIG 113. ABOVE AND RIGHT: 'Watteau' style cotton evening dress, Horrockses Fashions, *c.*1956. The Harris (2024.6).

FIG 114. Woman's dress, late eighteenth century. Victoria and Albert Museum.

The Horrockses' gown, meanwhile, pushes this historic reference further back, drawing a visual connection to the elaborate drapery of the eighteenth-century *robe à la française*, with its flowing back pleats and structured grace (114).

Collectively, these garments illustrate how the ideals of couture permeated beyond the ateliers of Paris. They affirm the potency of couture craftsmanship while highlighting the ingenuity of ready-to-wear brands like Horrockses in making these styles available to a broader public.

FIG 115. 'Hermacelles' dress, Hermès Paris, 1952.

The illusion of Hermès

> 'Everything in the dresses is an illusion – pockets, collars, buttons are all printed on in carefully haphazard strokes; only the seams are real.'[14]

Launched as part of Horrockses Fashions' Summer 1953 collection, the 'Great Illusion' dress (117) stands as a compelling example of mid-century fashion's engagement with *trompe l'oeil* techniques and the flow of design ideas between haute couture and ready-to-wear. The design was a licensed adaptation of a concept first introduced by the prestigious French maison Hermès in 1952, whose original 'Hermeselle' dress employed painted optical illusions to subvert the expectations of tailoring and embellishment (115).

In Horrockses' iteration, the revere collar, patch pockets and buttons are screen-printed onto a straight-cut cotton poplin dress, using painterly brushstrokes. The *Manchester Evening News* commented on the novelty of the design in May 1953:

> At last a Lancashire firm has provided the answer to the wilting collar or the pockets which are difficult to iron ... Although at first glance it looks as if the wearer is stepping out in a smartly tailored shirtwaister with big patch pockets, in reality she is wearing a simple V-necked cotton with no pockets or additional trimming at all.[15]

This journalistic fascination with the garment's illusionistic qualities points to a broader cultural moment. *Trompe l'oeil* has a long-standing art historical lineage, but its application within fashion reached a watershed moment in 1927, when Elsa Schiaparelli (1890–1973) debuted her now-iconic sweater featuring a *trompe l'oeil* bow and scarf motif (116). Schiaparelli's design initiated a dialogue between visual wit and sartorial construction that would be echoed decades later in both the Hermès' and Horrockses' designs.

Hermès' 'Hermeselle' dress was celebrated in European and American fashion circles. In the USA, the dress was licensed by New York dressmaker Herbert Sondheim (1895–1966), who adapted the model for the American market. In Britain, Horrockses Fashions obtained the rights to reproduce the design (117). While priced at a modest £5 to £6, a figure that aligned with

FIG 116. ABOVE: Jumper-cravat by Elsa Schiaparelli, Paris, France, early twentieth century. Victoria and Albert Museum.

FIG 117. RIGHT: Hermès of Paris and Horrockses of London announcement leaflet, 1953. Lancashire Archives (DDVC/ACC 7340/Box 9/3).

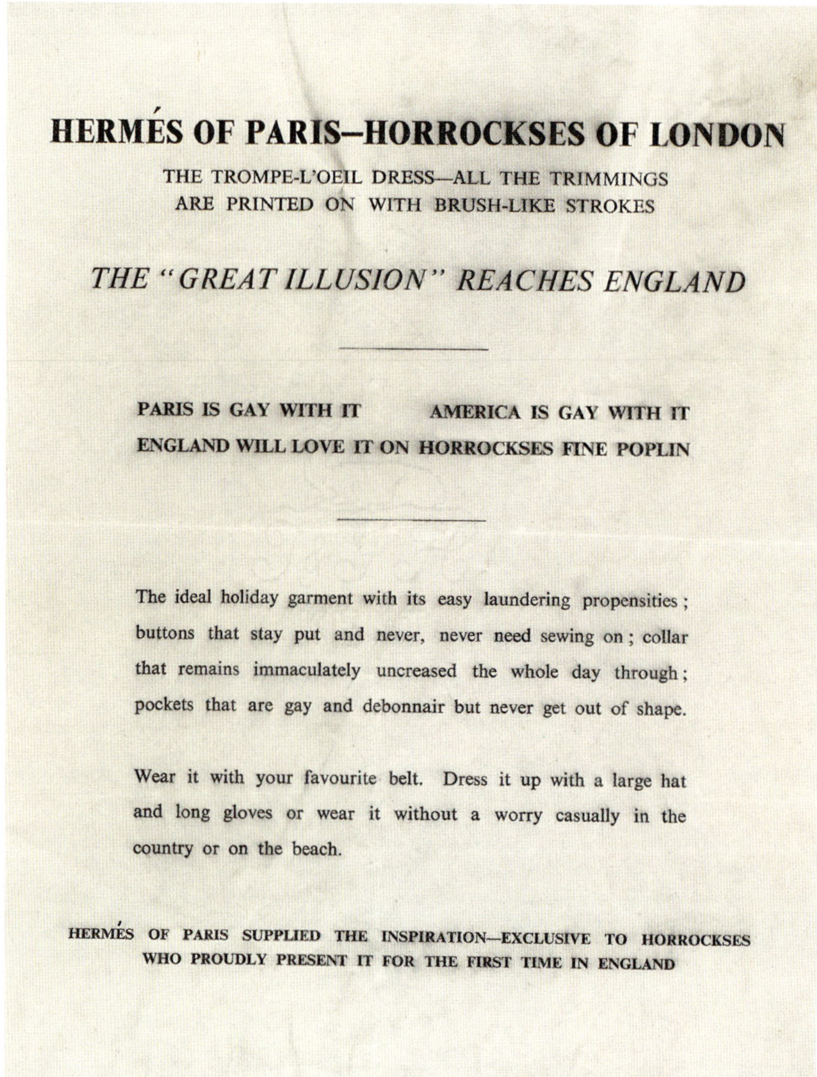

HERMÉS OF PARIS–HORROCKSES OF LONDON

THE TROMPE-L'OEIL DRESS—ALL THE TRIMMINGS
ARE PRINTED ON WITH BRUSH-LIKE STROKES

THE "GREAT ILLUSION" REACHES ENGLAND

PARIS IS GAY WITH IT AMERICA IS GAY WITH IT
ENGLAND WILL LOVE IT ON HORROCKSES FINE POPLIN

The ideal holiday garment with its easy laundering propensities; buttons that stay put and never, never need sewing on; collar that remains immaculately uncreased the whole day through; pockets that are gay and debonnair but never get out of shape.

Wear it with your favourite belt. Dress it up with a large hat and long gloves or wear it without a worry casually in the country or on the beach.

HERMÉS OF PARIS SUPPLIED THE INSPIRATION—EXCLUSIVE TO HORROCKSES WHO PROUDLY PRESENT IT FOR THE FIRST TIME IN ENGLAND

Horrockses' accessible market positioning, the original Hermès' versions commanded a far higher price point of 18 guineas.[16]

The Horrockses' version was adapted from the original by Tullis, whose sketch survives in the designer's notebooks now in the collection at The Harris Museum (118). While the original fabric swatch is missing, precluding a detailed technical analysis of the print's texture and method, the sketch provides key visual evidence of the interplay between dress structure and printed ornamentation.

This design illustrates not only the aesthetic versatility of Horrockses Fashions, but also the way in which mass-market British fashion could act as a conduit for sophisticated design ideas originating from the Parisian couture system.

FIG 118. Design book sketch of Horrockses' adaptation of the 'Hermacelles' dress, 1953.

Christian Dior

A blue-and-white floral strapless evening dress exemplifies Horrockses Fashions' innovative efforts to elevate ready-to-wear during the 1950s (120). Constructed from a white ground cotton fabric printed with a striking blue iris motif, the design features a full, gathered skirt, a boned bodice and a coordinating sash. The dress was designed by Tullis for Horrockses Fashions' Spring/Summer 1954 collection.

Both the textile design and the silhouette closely resemble a couture evening gown created by Christian Dior for his 'Ligne Tulipe' collection in 1953 (119, 121). Horrockses' adaptation demonstrates the brand's astute responsiveness to contemporary Parisian couture and encapsulates its broader design ethos: the merging of aspirational elegance with practical affordability.

While the 'Ligne Tulipe' collection takes its name from the distinctive silhouette of a tulip bloom, it also reflects Dior's profound and lifelong devotion to flowers. Florals were

FIG 119. 'Ligne Tulipe' by Christian Dior, 1953.

not merely decorative for Dior, but served as a conceptual foundation through which he explored volume, texture and femininity. He said: 'I designed my clothes for flower-like women, with rounded shoulders, full feminine busts, and hand-span waists above enormous spreading skirts.'[17]

Dior's strapless gown is constructed from white silk. It has a full-length voluminous skirt, a boned bodice and a dramatic sash that can be worn in a variety of different ways, forming soft, cascading folds which echo the gown's floral print of abstracted blue bouquets.

The striking parallel between the gowns cannot be underestimated. A comparative analysis reveals that the Horrockses' version closely follows many of the design elements of the Dior original. The dresses share a cinched waist and a full-length skirt. The strapless bodice with its gently curved, crossover sweetheart neckline is virtually identical in both garments, attesting to the faithful adaptation of key visual features. In Dior's couture version, a separate, free-flowing sash creates a dramatic sense of movement. In contrast, the Horrockses' gown integrates this sash into the bodice's structure, attaching it securely and lining it with blue cotton, a practical adaptation that reflects the economies of scale and material constraints typical of ready-to-wear. Even the textile design offers a further point of comparison: Dior's painterly blue floral silk, ethereal in its abstracted, falling blooms, is reinterpreted in the Horrockses' version through printed cotton, retaining a similar sense of visual dynamism, albeit rendered in more cost-effective fabric.

Such comparisons illustrate how Horrockses Fashions used the principles of haute couture, thoughtfully distilling them for the ready-to-wear market. They encourage a dialogue between couture and ready-to-wear and the ways in which elite design ideals shaped the visual and material culture of everyday dress.

Victor Stiebel

An evening gown, dating to 1954, in the collection at Manchester Art Gallery, offers another connection between Horrockses and the world of couture. Designed by London couturier Victor Stiebel (1907–1976), the gown pairs a striking full-length skirt in bold windowpane check with a sculpted white bodice. The check fabric has been expertly cut on the bias, creating dynamic diagonal lines that enhance the fluidity and movement of the silhouette.

FIG 120. ABOVE: Blue iris print dress, Horrockses Fashions, 1954. The Harris (2005.38).

FIG 121. RIGHT: Tulip dress by Christian Dior, 1953.

FIG 122. Cotton couture dress by Victor Steibel, 1954.

The structured, boned bodice evokes the corseted elegance of the period, while a matching stole, also cut on the bias, completes the ensemble with a sense of visual cohesion and theatrical grace (122).

Stiebel was a British couturier whose work defined a classically elegant and refined vision of mid-twentieth-century fashion. Born in South Africa, Stiebel established his couture house in London in 1932 and quickly became recognised for his graceful, polished silhouettes and understated opulence. In the post-war years, Stiebel played a key role in shaping a distinctively British couture sensibility, rooted in tradition but enlivened by contemporary verve and immaculate craftsmanship.

Although couture in spirit, this dress was created entirely in cotton for a Cotton Board fashion parade, demonstrating Stiebel's ability to elevate humble materials through technical mastery and design sophistication.

When viewed alongside a ready-to-wear evening dress by Horrockses Fashions, a compelling visual dialogue emerges. Both gowns share a similar aesthetic sensibility, employing bold graphic patterning to articulate the silhouette and create visual drama. The emphasis on a cinched waist and voluminous skirt places both designs firmly within the prevailing mid-century fashion ideal.

Yet, despite their surface similarities, the distinctions between couture and ready-to-wear are revealed in their construction and fabrication. Stiebel's gown, while made from cotton, relies on couture techniques such as internal boning and precise bias cutting to achieve its sculptural effect. The Horrockses' dress, surprisingly, reverses the expected hierarchy of materials: the bodice is crafted from luxurious black silk faille, while the full skirt is formed in plaid nylon organza (123). Unlike Stiebel's corseted bodice, the Horrockses' design favours a softer, more wearable silhouette suitable for mass production and a broader consumer market.

Both garments demonstrate a theatrical use of surface design, intended to captivate from a distance, yet they inhabit different realms of fashion culture. Stiebel's gown represents the rarefied world of couture, while the Horrockses' dress adapts similar stylistic and structural cues for a middle-class audience eager to participate in the elegance of post-war fashion. In their interplay, the two dresses offer insight into how ideas of glamour and modern femininity were expressed across various tiers of the fashion system.

FIG 123. Design for a cotton couture dress by Victor Steibel. Horrockses Fashions design book, 1954

Visual brand language

Horrockses Fashions strategically employed the visual language of haute couture to elevate the status of its ready-to-wear garments, particularly through the use of fashion illustration and photography. Its promotional strategies deliberately evoked the exclusivity and refinement associated with luxury. In doing so, Horrockses sought to bridge the gap between mass-market accessibility and elite fashion imagery, crafting a brand identity that aspired to the elegance of high fashion.

FIG 124. Cotton cocktail dress with black-and-red abstract rose design with cummerbund and sash trimmed with wool fringe, Horrockses Fashions, *c.*1956. The Harris (2025.7).

FIG 125. OPPOSITE: Horrockses' department store display cards, *c.*1955. Illustrations by Andrew Robb. The Harris (2003.53.1-4).

Central to this visual strategy was the work of British fashion illustrator Andrew Robb (1907–1989), a pivotal figure in twentieth-century fashion communication. Born in Leith, Scotland, Robb trained at Edinburgh College of Art, graduating in 1926, and began his career within commercial art studios before establishing himself as one of Britain's leading fashion illustrators. Known for his sensitive and dynamic renderings of contemporary fashion, Robb was recruited by the *Daily Express*, where he remained for nearly five decades.

Robb's reputation within the industry granted him regular access to international fashion collections and led to freelance commissions from numerous fashion houses, including Norman Hartnell. His illustrations for Horrockses Fashions captured the grace and poise typically reserved for couture, positioning Horrockses' garments within a stylistic register more commonly associated with the elite salons of Paris and London.

Robb's images (125), with their elongated figures, refined gestures and elegant stylisation, imbued Horrockses' designs with a sense of glamour and individuality. His work for Horrockses Fashions exemplifies how the brand cultivated an aspirational identity, using the tools of high fashion to mediate its place within the broader fashion system.

By the early 1950s, fashion photography had begun to surpass illustration as the principal means of promoting and communicating sartorial style. At the forefront of this visual transformation was John French (1907–1966), a pioneering British fashion photographer whose elegant, technically distinctive images came to define the look of mid-century fashion.

Trained originally as a commercial artist, French brought a compositional clarity and graphic sensibility to his photographic work. His signature use of diffused natural light and low-contrast exposures was developed in part to accommodate the print quality of newsprint, allowing his images to retain detail and tonal subtlety when reproduced in the popular press.

French's collaboration with Horrockses Fashions during the 1950s was especially significant in shaping the public image of the brand (126, 127). His images elevated the garments beyond their commercial reality and positioned them within a visual language that referenced the sophistication of Parisian couture.

A particularly striking example is seen in French's photograph of a model wearing a Horrockses Fashions' fitted,

Horrockses

Horrockses

Horrockses

Horrockses

FIG 126. A pencil-skirt suit by Horrockses Fashions, 1950s. Photographed by John French. The Harris Museum (2011.122).

check-patterned suit with a cinched waist, three-quarter sleeves and accentuated hip line, a silhouette recalling Dior's 'New Look'. The model's pose, angled with arms extended and gloved hands drawing attention to the silhouette's architectural precision, speaks to the photographer's skill in highlighting both the construction and the poise of the ensemble. The monochromatic tonality, offset by the interplay of textures, showcases French's mastery of light and contrast. This was not merely fashion photography but an act of aesthetic storytelling, translating the democratic appeal of Horrockses into images that suggested exclusivity and high style. French's work for Horrockses helped construct a compelling visual identity for one of Britain's most influential ready-to-wear labels.

Horrockses Fashions occupies a distinctive position in the history of twentieth-century British fashion. Emerging from a

FIG 127. A full-skirted Horrockses Fashions' dress with an abstract print, 1956. Photographed by John French.

cotton manufacturing legacy yet driven by the desire to align with the rarefied world of haute couture, the brand successfully bridged the divide between industry and artistry. By consciously embedding itself within the structures, aesthetics and marketing strategies of couture through its location, design practices and marketing aesthetic, Horrockses Fashions cultivated an image of refined exclusivity that was at odds with its ready-to-wear status.

This strategic alignment with Parisian and London couture was not merely aspirational, but central to the brand's identity. From the adaptation of silhouettes seen in the couture shows to the salon-like presentation of collections in its Hanover Square townhouse, Horrockses consistently evoked the rituals and spaces of high fashion. Designers with couture training, such as John Tullis, played a key role in ensuring that even mass-produced garments retained an air of sophistication and craft. The production of 'Specials' further blurred the boundaries between couture and ready-to-wear, cementing the label's dual appeal to both exclusivity and accessibility.

In the broader cultural landscape of post-war Britain, Horrockses Fashions offered a compelling sartorial proposition: high-style clothing made from everyday fabrics, grounded in domestic industry yet styled with international flair. It promised women not only elegance but also modern garments that reflected the optimism, femininity and upward mobility of the 1950s.

Horrockses Fashions' success reveals much about the shifting dynamics of taste, class and fashion consumption in the mid-twentieth century and about how the language of couture could be reinterpreted to suit the aspirations of a new, increasingly style-conscious public. In doing so, Horrockses Fashions expanded the possibilities of British ready-to-wear, proving that mass-produced fashion could be chic and still carry the imprint of elegance, exclusivity and design integrity.

8 HORROCKSES FASHIONS Sample Sheets

SCOTT SCHIAVONE

Preserved within the Horrockses Fashions archive at The Harris are 240 sample sheets, acquired in 2011, dating to 1955–59. These documents offer a rare insight into the processes that transformed a designer's concept into a finished, mass-produced garment.

Each sheet records a single dress design and typically includes a sketch of the garment and a swatch of the intended fabric. The sheets also contain technical and commercial information, such as the garment's style number, sizes and wholesale price. This combination of creative and administrative detail reveals how Horrockses carefully balanced design, manufacturing and retail.

Produced in the sampling room at the company's London headquarters, these sheets functioned as instructions for the mills responsible for making up the garments. There, the machinists translated the designs into finished garments. One such site was Ivy Mill in Manchester, part of the network of textile production that supported the Horrockses' brand.

These sample sheets provide an invaluable record of the company's production system. They play an important role in identifying and dating garments. This is the first time these rare archival materials have been reproduced in print.

FIG 128. PP. 153–63: A selection of sample sheets dating from 1955 to 1959, Horrockses Fashions. The Harris (2011.114).

STYLE NO. G. 172
IM. NO. 4206
PRICE
SIZES 10-16
R.S.P.

COL. 1

CO

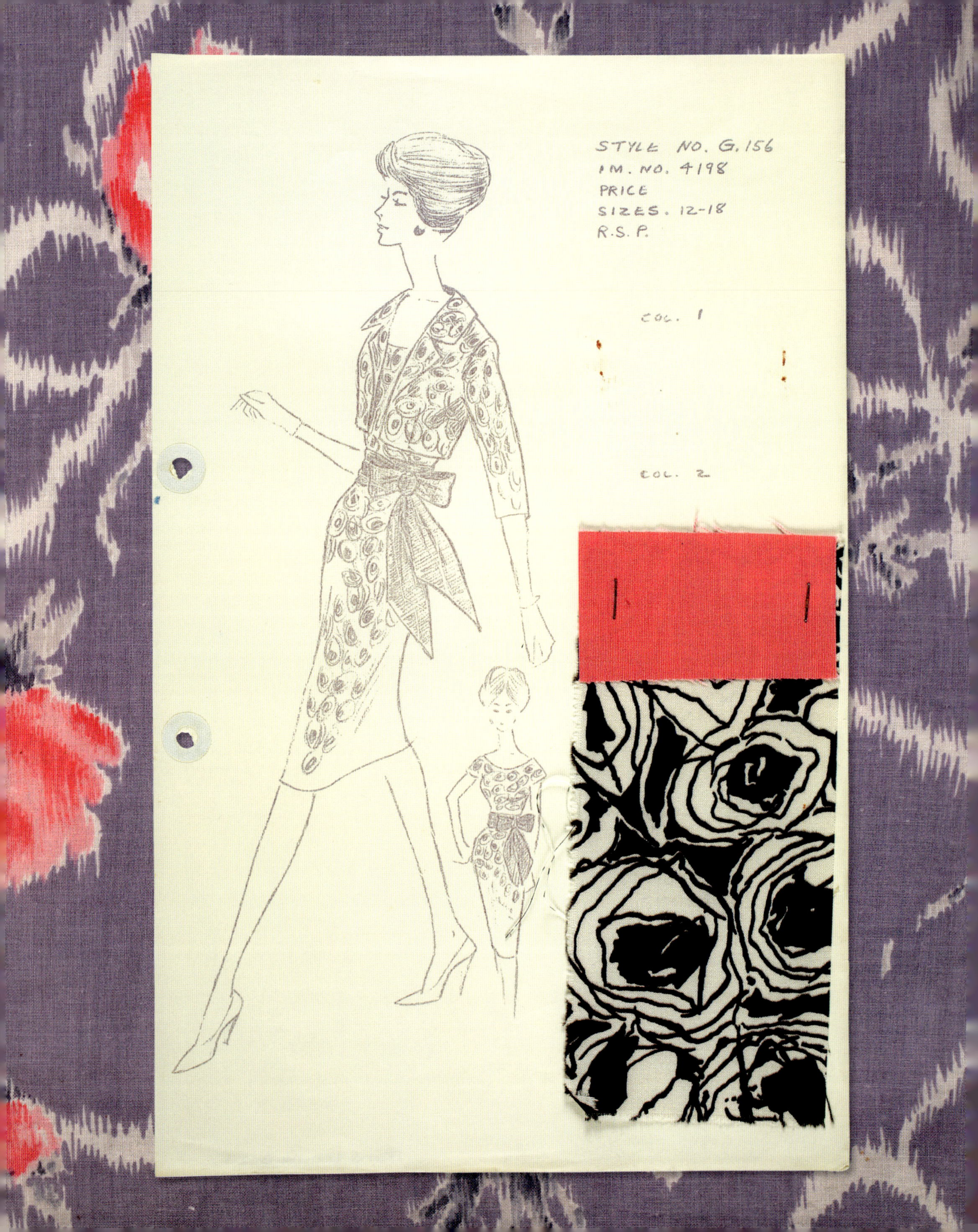
STYLE NO. G.156
IM. NO. 4198
PRICE
SIZES. 12-18
R.S.P.
COL. 1
COL. 2

STYLE NO. J. 329
IM. 4382
PRICE
SIZES. 10-16
R.S.P.
COL. 1
COL. 2

STYLE NO. G. 281
IM. NO. 4167
PRICE
SIZE 12-16
R.S.P.
COL. 1

STYLE NO. J. 361
IM. 4375
PRICE
SIZES. 10-16
R.S.P.
COL. 1
COL. 2

STYLE NO. J. 87
IM. 5755
PRICE
SIZES 12-20
R.S.P.

STYLE NO. J. 117
IM. 4360
PRICE
SIZES. 10-16
R.S.P.

STYLE NO. J. 103
IM. 5810
PRICE
SIZES. 10-16
R.S.P.

STYLE NO. J. 349
IM. 4301
PRICE
SIZES. 12-20
R.S.P.
col. 4

STYLE NO. G. 177
IM. NO. 4226
PRICE
SIZES. 10-18
R.S.P.
COL. 1
COL. 2
COL. 3

IM. 4366
PRICE
SIZES. 10-18
R.S.P.
COL. 1
COL. 2

STYLE NO. G. 302
K. 251
CONTRAST 3354
PRICE
SIZES. 10-16
R.S.P.
COL. 1
CONTRAST
COL. 101

STYLE NO. G. 183.
IM. NO. 4129
PRICE
SIZES 10-16
R.S.P.
COL 1
COL. 2
COL. 3

STYLE NO. J. 134
IM. 3843
PRICE
SIZES. 12–18
R.S.P.
COL 1
COL. 4

STYLE NO. J. 122
IM. 4282
PRICE
SIZES. 10–18
R.S.P.
COL 1
COL. 2

STYLE NO. J. 317
IM 4403
PRICE
SIZES 10–18
R.S.P
COL 1
COL. 4

STYLE NO. G. 189
IM. NO. 4177
PRICE
SIZES. 10-14
R.S.P.
COL. 1
COL. 2

STYLE NO. G. 191
IM. NO. 4185
PRICE
SIZES. 10-16
R.S.P.
COL. 1
COL. 2

STYLE NO. G. 159
IM. NO. 5578
PRICE
SIZES. 10-18
R.S.P.
COL. 13
COL. 14

STYLE NO. J. 59
IM. 4351
PRICE
SIZES. 10-16
R.S.P.
COL 1

STYLE NO. G. 160
IM. NO. 5581
PRICE
SIZES. 10-16
R.S.P.
COL. 910
COL. 911

9 LOVED, WORN, REMEMBERED
Horrockses Fashions through the Eyes of Collectors

LIZ TREGENZA AND NADINE COYNE

Liz Tregenza is an academic based at London College of Fashion and a vintage dealer who has been wearing and selling Horrockses' garments since 2008. Nadine Coyne is a Preston-based vintage collector. This interview was conducted over two sessions in summer 2025, firstly online and then when Liz went to visit Nadine in Preston to look at some of the pieces in her personal collection. The interview focuses primarily on Horrockses Fashions' pieces produced between 1946 and the early 1960s.

FIG 129. Pink cotton dress with white stripes with blue squggle pattern and cotton day dress with pink stripes with purple, yellow, green and blue floral pattern. Both dresses by Horrockses Fashions, *c.*1948. Textiles designed by Alistair Morton. The Harris (2020.17.1 and 2020.17.4).

LT Can you tell me how you first got into vintage clothing?

NC I first got into vintage when I was about 15 years old, so it would be the late 1970s. I used to go to Manchester and London, and I would buy vintage blouses. I'd buy the granny coats and the little 1950s jackets that were all nipped in, which I loved. But even going back further, I remember being eight years old and becoming interested in fashion for the first time. At our school, we didn't have uniforms; we wore our own clothes, which must have been a nightmare for parents. I loved it because I could wear what I wanted. And I used to have the dagger collars and the chevrons. Then, at 15, I got a job as a Saturday girl at Chelsea Girl. From then on, fashion was what I loved.

LT And what about Horrockses' garments specifically – when did you start buying those?

NC It was around 2007 or 2008 when I started

wearing vintage again. I'd had my children and lost my way a bit fashion-wise: you're just in survival mode, and you're going to work and haven't got time for yourself. But once I'd come out of the fog of bringing up young children, I found myself again and started dressing for me. I started collecting my vintage again and wearing Horrockses. You could pick up dresses for about £60 – amazing, compared to today.

LT Do you have any recollection of which Horrockses' dress you bought first?

NC I can't remember which was my very first one, but soon after I started buying vintage again, I found the internet and that opened up this bigger world of Horrockses.

LT We started buying Horrockses at roughly the same time. They were quite cheap then! I was buying most of the early ones on eBay. Where were you picking them up?

NC Yes, eBay was the easy one, and you could still go to Manchester and find them, and you could look in charity shops for them, too.

LT Have you ever bought a Horrockses in a charity shop?

NC I've had one from a charity shop and that was through Debra about eight years ago (130). She messaged me and said, 'Nadine, there's a Horrockses in our local charity shop and I think it's your size and it's about £30'. So, I said, 'Debra, it doesn't matter if it doesn't fit me – if it's a Horrockses for only £30, just buy it!' It was a fruit print one with a greyish background – quite a famous design. That was the cheapest I ever bought.

LT That's so funny. I can't remember how much I paid for all of my Horrockses now. But you do remember both the very cheap and the very expensive ones.

NC Yes! You remember the iconically [*sic*] cheap and the iconically [*sic*] eye-watering!

LT In the early days of buying Horrockses

FIG 130. Nadine wearing a grey fruit-print Horrockses' dress, purchased from a charity shop.

FIG 131. A close-up of Nadine's Horrockses' skirts with prints by Ursula Hertz.

I know you were buying mostly online, on sites like eBay, but did you also make some in-person purchases?

NC Of course, I bought some from Emma at the Looking Glass [a vintage shop in Bridgnorth, Shropshire]. She always kept her eye out for me, saying, 'Nadine, I've got one I think you'll like'.

LT I've bought some lovely pieces from the Looking Glass, too.

NC But I never went, oh, I've got to buy a Horrockses. I had to really like it.

LT Yes, so not just collecting for the sake of collecting.

NC First and foremost I'm a wearer. I have to be able to wear them.

LT At one point I was a collector. I had over 200 Horrockses' pieces. I don't have anywhere near that many now. Today, mine are primarily for wearing, and increasingly over the years I've sold off the ones that weren't my size because I wanted to let them back out into the wild again to be loved and worn.

Are there specific styles and designs of Horrockses that you're particularly drawn to?

NC I love Alastair Morton's prints, especially the ones that make you feel like you're under the sea.

LT That's interesting. I always think of his prints as florals, but I can see how they have an under-the-sea quality to them. They kind of look like jellyfish.

If I were to think about what is a very 'Nadine' print, I would have probably said the Pat Albeck prints, the bold florals with the dark lines.

NC Yes, but sometimes you can't resist the wilder and the wackier ones, like the newspaper print with the flowers.

LT Yes, that's Pat Albeck.

NC The other print designer I love is Ursula Hertz. I've got two skirts with the most incredible prints. All sorts of unusual elements – one has hand gestures on it. And the combination of colours too – it shouldn't work, but it does (131).

LT Oh, yes, I have some of hers. So, you're drawn more to the bolder prints, rather than the plainer pieces Horrockses made?

NC Yes.

LT Do you have preferred silhouettes, too? Horrockses made a real variety of silhouettes, from the pencil-slim wiggle dresses to those with the big full skirts.

NC I like the dresses with fitted bodices, cinched in at the waist and then the skirt flowing out.

LT Yes, I love a full skirt.

NC As I've got older, I prefer a minimum 26-inch (66 cm) length, so it hits just below my knee, let's call it ballerina length. I feel that's so elegant, even with ballet pumps. Or if you're going out, you can dress it up. It's like you're in the 1950s. Do you know what I mean?

LT Yes. I do. The ballerina-length ones are so lovely, so feminine.

NC Another thing that gets me is that the pattern matching is sublime on Horrockses' pieces (132).

LT It's so lovely, isn't it? For me it comes from my background. I trained as a fashion designer. I understand how garments are made and that it costs more to pattern match something properly. Horrockses' garments are always so carefully thought out. It must have been expensive making them up so that all the elements matched perfectly.

I wanted to revisit something you said earlier, about the fit of Horrockses' dresses. I definitely remember when I first started buying Horrockses' pieces, more so than with many other brands, that the sundresses seemed to fit me like a glove, with the perfect bust to waist ratio, although I do often have to alter the straps. What do you think about the fit?

NC Yes. The sundresses fit beautifully and they really do flatter the figure, whereas I find the shirtwaisters very long-bodied.

LT They are, aren't they? The summer dresses with the little boleros feel like they're more suited to a shorter person, and the shirtwaisters are much better if you are taller.

NC I totally agree. It's very rare to find a Horrockses' shirtwaister with less than a 17-inch (43 cm) bodice.

LT I have one that someone had taken in through the shoulder seams and made it much shorter. But I only need a 15-inch (38 cm) bodice, so I always struggle with shirtwaisters.

NC Yes, ditto.

LT Although, even saying all of this, I often wear the sundresses without their boleros. Sometimes I feel that's a bit much! I love the sundresses because of how they fit me, but there's also something about how the prints work together. Many Horrockses' designs have this really clever engineering of prints and how they work across the dress. So, you have a print that has been used slightly differently on the bodice and the skirt, for example. I have a fabulous dress from 1953, with pink roses, that does this. It featured in an advertisement for Quintafix (133).

NC Oh yes. They blend beautifully. Also, those dresses you see from the front that are lovely, but which you turn around and go, wow! It's such a nice surprise when you see interesting back detail, like the waterfall backs. Gorgeous! (134).

LT Oh, yes, the waterfall design – I call it a Watteau back, like the eighteenth-century dresses. So many Horrockses have clever back designs, like bow or strap details, or backs that are a little bit lower than average, which is really chic and stylish (135).

I was interested that you mentioned Alastair Morton. He was one of the earliest textile designers to work with Horrockses Fashions in the 1940s, but many of his textiles are used for garments that have slightly different silhouettes to our 'preferred' ones – lots of housecoats, for example.

NC I love housecoats as well. Look at them compared to what we call dressing gowns today. Each one is different. I've got the double crossover ones and the ones with batwing sleeves. There's so much material in them. And they're just so comfy to sit there in, but also they make you glide. They don't make you want to put on a big pair of fluffy socks. I wear mine with ballet pumps. They make you feel glamorous (136).

LT Yes! There's something about the length, cut and volume of fabric. But I suppose that's something so key about most Horrockses' cotton pieces, isn't it? It's the volume of fabric in them.

NC Yes, it's unbelievable.

FIG 132. One of Nadine's Horrockses' dresses with careful pattern matching.

FIG 133. Liz wearing a 1953 rose-print Horrockses' dress.

FIG 134. A back view of one of Nadine's Horrockses' dresses.

FIG 135. Liz wearing one of her 'Watteau back' Horrockses' dresses.

LT Thinking about other brands I've collected, which were operating in the same period, there's nothing quite like a Horrockses for the sheer volume of fabric used.

NC That's a really good quote – there's nothing quite like a Horrockses!

LT I wonder if this comes down to when the brand was established and what Horrockses was trying to achieve in the late 1940s and early 1950s. Other ready-to-wear companies weren't scrimping necessarily, but it seems like Horrockses was using as much fabric as it possibly could in a design.

NC Nobody matches them, no. You put your Horrockses on and feel the fullness. I don't think any other brand has ever come close to it.

LT Of course, you can figure this out by taking measurements, but I'd be really interested to see a Horrockses' sundress or skirt unpicked, just to get a visual understanding of how much fabric was used.

NC The Ursula Hertz skirts came to me unpicked. There was a lot of fabric in them and they were in pieces. We aren't sure what the previous owner had in mind for them, but Melanie fitted them back together.

LT Oh, amazing. That leads me onto another question. Do you ever have things altered to fit?

NC I'm loathe to have garments altered. Sometimes I'll wear a belt on top if it's a little bit big. I do also have some pieces that have clearly been altered in the past.

LT When I started collecting Horrockses' pieces, I did have some altered to fit. But I stopped a few years ago, and now I only ever alter the straps or the length: alterations that can be reversed easily. I feel the way Horrockses' dresses are made, the straps are there to be altered – there's always such a long 'tail' in the spaghetti-strap dresses.

NC Yes. You can do it easily.

FIG 136. Nadine wearing one of her Horrockses' housecoats.

LT If they are still their original size, I'm disinclined to start fiddling around with them. I'd only be tempted by a print I'd never seen before, or felt I was never likely to see again. But even so, I'd try to ensure the alterations were easily reversible. There's something special about buying the unaltered pieces.

NC I know. Yes. And it's not often you find an original, unaltered. Some previous owners made bad little tweaks, but also sometimes good tweaks.

LT I've bought some wonderful pieces that haven't been worn at all. There's one skirt I'm thinking of where I got into a bidding war on eBay and spent a lot of money.

NC It was against me, wasn't it?

LT That pink one, with the advertisements? I think it's an Ursula Hertz design as well? That's the one I mean. I adore that skirt. I've worn it so much (137).

There's a decent-sized group of collectors who really love Horrockses, and for the prints that don't come up very often, the bidding will go up and up, and you'll be like, 'I'm committed now. I've said I'm going to do this and I'm keeping going!'

NC Yes!

LT That skirt came to me pristine. It was so crisp and the cotton had this amazing sheen to it, like it had never been washed – it still seemed shop fresh. It's an incredible feeling sometimes when you buy something vintage and think, how has this existed for 60-ish years and no one has worn it?

NC But you find that with a lot of Horrockses' pieces, don't you – how good they still look, how fresh the cotton is. I put some of mine in the washing machine because they're cotton.

LT Me too!

NC They hold up so well, though. I'm sure people in the 1950s would have washed them in all sorts of ways.

LT I assume most people would have hand-washed them. Horrockses' garments wash really well – the dye fastness is excellent – whereas I've had awful instances with other vintage pieces where the colours have run when I've put them in the washing machine.

NC Horrockses never do, do they? You put them on the washing line and bingo! And they iron so beautifully. It's such a treat, actually, to iron a Horrockses' dress. When the pleats are all pressed out, I actually go a bit weak at the knees!

LT I know what you mean. It's the weight and the quality of the cotton. Every Horrockses' dress I have, no matter whether it's sort of visibly tired looking or not, the cotton feels beautiful. There's something about some of my Horrockses' pieces that have obviously been heavily worn and clearly appreciated – there's a lovely softness to them, too.

FIG 137. Liz wearing her Ursula Hertz print Horrockses' skirt.

NC Yes! You get that with some vintage pieces, which have that worn-out tired look to them, but Horrockses don't look like that. They don't look tired. They just look loved. And they don't fall apart. You don't wear out Horrockses, do you?

LT No. The only thing that happens, and this is probably because I love things being a bit tighter than I should, is that I have popped open quite a lot of seams around zips and had to hand-stitch them back up.

When I find an unaltered Horrockses with an Aero Zip I'm always delighted. Those zips are so good and strong. I think that's the reason why so many vintage collectors are drawn to them. Every element of a Horrockses' dress is quality. Everything is carefully designed and everything stands the test of time: the deep hems you can easily turn down, or the generous seam allowances that can be let out. There's the odd print that you don't love, but Horrockses' garments are so timeless, especially the prints. You know it's a 1950s dress, but I never find a Horrockses aggressively twee in a way I do when I look at some of the clothing made by other companies that were operating at the same time.

NC Yes, as you said, timeless and classic.

LT I must have been 18 when I bought my first Horrockses, and I'm still wearing the same ones and loving them in my mid-30s. I feel Horrockses can look fabulous on a 17- to 18-year-old, and also on a 70-year-old.

NC Yes. I look at what you wear and I think, I would wear it in almost the same way, other than sometimes you might pop a little denim jacket on, whereas I'll maybe add a vintage jacket or a shirt tied over the top. I often wear the dresses with my Converse.

LT I sometimes wear mine with trainers, too. In the past, I wore lots of authentic period looks – the hats, shoes, hair – but I wear them quite differently now, perhaps more casually, with flat fisherman sandals in the summer or with black tights and my black patent Doc Martens in the winter. I love wearing summer dresses throughout the year. You just have to think about how you can style them to keep wearing them, basically. They can be worn in many different ways by different people.

NC I tend to wear more 1940s pieces in winter, but I do keep a few Horrockses out in case an occasion comes up – a wedding, or somebody's party – because you know you can just put them on, and in winter you can add a bolero or a jacket. You still look good and feel good. I do love it when spring comes around and you can get them all out again, though.

LT Yes, absolutely. You mentioned weddings – almost every wedding I've been to as an adult, I've worn a Horrockses' dress.

FIG 138. Liz wearing a Horrockses' unit print dress, designed by John Tullis in 1958.

FIG 139. Cotton summer dress with yellow roses, Horrockses Fashions, *c.*1958. The Harris (2001.36).

NC I feel like I've got to because no other dress comes close.

LT Horrockses are the perfect wedding-guest dress. You feel great, but you've also not gone too fancy or too bridal.

NC Yes!

LT There are certain Horrockses' designs that were so popular and seem to have survived so well – you see multiples of them. The 1954 Pat Albeck 'oranges and lemons' print, for example.

NC But they're like buses. You don't see any, and then suddenly three or four come along at once.

LT Absolutely. Do you have multiples of any of your Horrockses?

NC I've got a couple of prints that are in different colourways or styles.

LT Me too. There's one I've had in three colourways. I consider it one of the most iconic designs and it's one of my favourites, too. It's a John Tullis unit print dress from 1958 (138).

NC Yes, I've got that. Is it in turquoise and yellow?

LT I've got it in blue and yellow and I used to have it in pink. What have you got?

NC I've got it in lilac (140).

LT Lovely! It's such a great design. I now want to talk about the Preston connection, as you live in Preston and Horrockses has this Preston history. What are your thoughts on the local connection?

NC I love it! Back in the 1980s, me and my friend used to walk home after going to nightclubs and we'd walk past the Horrockses' mill. I was never taught about Horrockses, but it was always there in the background.

I grew up knowing about it through grandparents working in the mills. But none of mine ever worked at Horrockses because we were just outside Preston. We were in Leyland, which is only five minutes on the train to Preston, but you still think of Horrockses as in your hometown.

FIG 140. Nadine wearing the Cotton summer dress with roses in purple, Horrockses Fashions, *c.*1958.

If you go into Preston in a Horrockses, the older generation stop you and say, 'Oh, I had a dress similar to that'. Once you get onto 'it's a Horrockses', they say, 'Oh, my Auntie used to work in the mill!' There's always some story in Preston connected to Horrockses.

One of my friends, who is in her early 80s, remembers being able to go to Preston market and buy Horrockses' material to make up your own frocks. As to whether it was legitimate – well, I don't mean it was fake, but perhaps someone was procuring it when they shouldn't have been. There were no labels or anything!

LT Yes, I've heard stories like that. Maybe that's part of the reason why so many unlabelled Horrockses turn up on the vintage market.

NC Yes! If I go to The Harris Museum, I have to wear a Horrockses, because you're among them, so to speak.

LT Are any of the historic department stores

FIG 141. Nadine with Pat Coyne, her mum. Pat is wearing a Joanie × Horrockses' dress and Nadine's is an original.

in Preston, which were there in Horrockses' heyday, still there, or have they all gone now?

NC No. Sadly, the last of them closed during the Covid-19 pandemic and never reopened. The older businesses that would have been there have now gone. But a lot of old buildings still exist – you just have to look up. You've got the Miller Arcade and The Harris, of course.

LT Preston, like so much of Lancashire, has its cotton mill heritage.

NC Yes, and lots terraced houses, where the mill workers would have lived.

LT Yes, absolutely. There's something special about wearing Horrockses in Preston. While most of the dresses were made in Manchester, the cotton was woven in Preston.

NC If I see anybody in a Horrockses' dress, I have to tell them how lovely it is. When I buy one, I say to my husband, – and this is my mantra – I'm repatriating the dresses back to Preston (142).

LT I love that so much. Horrockses are always a talking point as well. More so than with a lot of other vintage garments I wear, I find that people stop me when I'm wearing a Horrockses' piece and want to talk to me about it.

NC Oh gosh, yes.

LT I'll often be asked if it's original, and my answer is always yes (143)!

That brings us nicely onto the question of reproduction versus original. Over the years there have been a number of Horrockses' relaunches, most notably the Joanie × Horrockses collaboration in 2022. Did you buy any pieces?

NC Yes, I did (141). Many people in the vintage world were worried about the relaunch. There was a lot of discussion about whether it would devalue the originals. But Joanie did a really good job. The garments were a nice length. They were made in cotton, the bodices were lined and they had cotton underskirts. Plus, they were accessible.

LT I agree. Because they changed the proportions of the prints, it was obvious that they weren't originals. For collectors and purists who wouldn't want to buy a repro, they were distinguishable from the originals.

But it's also about accessibility, isn't it? As we know, for some of the original garments you pay £200 to £300. That's out of the realm of what many people can afford, whereas the Joanie pieces were much more affordable and enabled people to buy into that style. The sizing was also fairly inclusive. Original Horrockses tend to turn up in smaller sizes. The Joanie styles allowed people to buy into the look who might typically be excluded.

FIG 142. Some favourites from Nadine's collection.

FIG 143. Liz and Nadine, both wearing Pat Albeck print Horrockses' dresses.

NOTES

Introduction Christine Boydell

1. 'Cotton concerto', *The Drapers' Record* (13 April 1946), pp. 46–47.
2. 'Cotton is the new fabric for fashion', *Evening Standard* (28 March 1946). Lancashire Archives, DDHs 49/1, 1940–46 Newscuttings Book.
3. *Inaugural Presentation of Fashions in Cotton*, 1946, Horrockses, Crewdson & Co. AAD/1995/16/12/1.
4. Ibid.
5. 'You can wear royal dresses', *Daily Sketch* (6 November 1953).
6. Boydell 2010.

From Mill to Museum Scott Schiavone

1. Interview with Maryse Addison, conducted by Christine Boydell, 15 June 2016.
2. Interview with Maryse Addison, conducted by Christine Boydell, 15th June 2016.

Tradition with Vision Lisa Mason

1. Horrockses, Crewdson & Co. Ltd, *The Cloth of the World* (Preston, 1938), p. 4. National Art Library Special Collections, 913298674.
2. Tregenza 2023.
3. Audrey Withers, 'Fashion, dress fabrics and accessories', in Council of Industrial Design 1946, p. 45.
4. 'Cool, crisp cottons', *Country Life* (10 May 1946), p. 872.
5. 'Preview to cotton', *The Ambassador*, no. 4 (1946), pp. 69–72. AAD/1987/1/13.
6. *Inaugural Presentation of Fashions in Cotton*, 1946, Horrockses, Crewdson & Co. AAD/1995/16/12/1.
7. Alison Settle, 'A woman's viewpoint', *The Observer* (9 November 1952). Brighton University Design Archives, A.52.43.
8. Boydell 2010, p. 45.
9. Boydell 2010.
10. Ibid., pp. 57–105.
11. Ibid., p. 41.
12. Ibid., p. 43.
13. Jackson, *Alastair Morton and Edinburgh Weavers*, 2012, p. 152.
14. Ibid., p. 160.
15. Jenny Lowndes, author interview, 2 May 2019.
16. Llewellyn 2015.
17. Klein 1965, pp. 33–37.
18. Boydell 2010, p. 42.
19. Pat Albeck archive, AAD/2004/9/75.
20. Pat Albeck archive, AAD/2004/9/81.
21. Christine Boydell, 'Free-lance textile design in the 1930s: an improving prospect?', *Journal of Design History*, vol. 8, no. 1 (1995), p. 27.
22. *The Herald* (14 March 1947). Joyce Badrocke archive, AAD/2009/4.
23. James de Holden Stone, reference letter, RCA, 19 July 1950. Joyce Badrocke archive, AAD/2009/4.
24. 'Chosen by Vogue', *Vogue* (January 1953). Joyce Badrocke archive, AAD/2009/4.
25. Joyce Badrocke, *Museum Themes in Print Design* (MA thesis, Royal College of Art, London, 1950), p. 1. Joyce Badrocke archive, AAD/2009/4.
26. Jackson, *From Atoms to Patterns*, 2012.
27. Juler 2016, p. 208.
28. Breward and Wilcox 2012.
29. 'Painting into Textiles', *The Ambassador*, no. 11 (1953), pp. 90–91.
30. Hans Juda, 'Introduction: Painting into Textiles', *The Ambassador*, no. 11 (1953), p. 73.
31. Cotton 2013.
32. Boydell 2010, p. 42.
33. Victoria and Albert Museum Collection: CIRC.71 to B-1947.
34. Boydell 2010, p. 95.
35. Council of Industrial Design 1946, p. 7.
36. Maguire and Woodham 1997; Atkinson 2012.
37. Pritchard 2009, pp. 9–25.
38. Hlaváčkova 2019, p. 63.
39. David Sassoon, 'Foreword', in Whitmore and Bide 2023, pp. 8–9.
40. Bohm-Duchen 2019.
41. The Harris Museum & Art Gallery, PRSMG:2011.111.8.
42. Herbert Loebl, *Government-financed Factories and the Establishment of Industries by Refugees in the Special Areas of the North of England 1937–1961* (M.Phil. thesis, Durham University, 1978).
43. Nyburg 2020, p. 55.
44. Ibid., p. 141.

Horrockses Fashions and the Legacy of Floral Femininity Paige Blake

1. Beth D. Charleston and Harold Koda, 'Christian Dior (1905–1957)', *Heilbrunn Timeline of Art History* (The Metropolitan Museum of Art, New York, 2004, updated 2023), https://www.metmuseum.org/toah/hd/dior/hd_dior.htm (accessed 6 June 2024).
2. 'Victorian dresses: styles, trends, and their cultural significance', *1883 Magazine* (6 December 2022), https://1883magazine.com/victorian-dresses-styles-trends-and-their-cultural-significance/ (accessed 22 November 2025).
3. Chertsey Museum, 'Blooming marvellous: flowers in fashion', https://chertseymuseum.org/BloomingMarvellous (accessed 17 October 2025).
4. Mackrell 1992, pp. 28, 23.
5. Burger 2011, p. 176.
6. Beth D. Charleston and Harold Koda, 'Christian Dior (1905–1957)', *Heilbrunn Timeline of Art History* (The Metropolitan Museum of Art, New York, 2004, updated 2023), https://www.metmuseum.org/toah/hd/dior/hd_dior.htm (accessed 6 June 2024).
7. Caroline C. Biggs, *'Hold that Hemline!': Christian Dior's New Look in America* (MA thesis, Sarah Lawrence College, Bronxville, NY, 2012), p. 3.
8. Caroline C. Biggs, *'Hold that Hemline!': Christian Dior's New Look in America* (MA thesis, Sarah Lawrence College, Bronxville, NY, 2012).
9. Information recorded from Mrs Knowles. The Harris Museum & Art Gallery, 2009.206.
10. Caroline C. Biggs, *'Hold that Hemline!': Christian Dior's New Look in America* (MA thesis, Sarah Lawrence College, Bronxville, NY, 2012), p. 6.
11. Caroline Elenowitz-Hess, 'Reconstructing the "femme-fleur": floral modernism in the work of Madeleine Vionnet and Jeanne Lanvin', *Journal of Design History*, vol. 35, no. 2 (2022), pp. 99–117, p. 99, https://doi.org/10.1093/jdh/epab035 (accessed 26 June 2025).
12. Chertsey Museum, 'Blooming marvellous: flowers in fashion', https://chertseymuseum.org/BloomingMarvellous (accessed 17 October 2025).
13. De la Haye 2020.
14. Boydell 2010.
15. Gipson 2022, p. 7.
16. Boydell 2010, p. 72.
17. De la Haye 2020, p. 13.

18. Information from object record file. The Harris Museum & Art Gallery, 2000.298.
19. Roux 2020, p. 54.
20. Edward Wigley and Vevila R.C. Dornelles, 'Blue is for boys: postfeminist continuations of gender, body and hue in UK magazines, 2009–2018', *Gender, Place & Culture*, vol. 29, no. 3 (2022), pp. 345–71, p. 365, https://doi.org/10.1080/0966369X.2021.1891864 (accessed 6 June 2024).
21. Veronika Koller, '"Not just a colour": pink as a gender and sexuality marker in visual communication', *Visual Communication*, vol. 7, no. 4 (2008), pp. 395–423, https://doi.org/10.1177/1470357208096209 (accessed 7 July 2024).
22. Caroline Elenowitz-Hess, 'Reconstructing the "femme-fleur": floral modernism in the work of Madeleine Vionnet and Jeanne Lanvin', *Journal of Design History*, vol. 35, no. 2 (2021), pp. 99–117, https://doi.org/10.1093/jdh/epab035 (accessed 6 June 2024).
23. Steele 2010, p. 21.
24. Amanda Fortini, 'The enduring appeal of Laura Ashley', *The New York Times* (21 October 2021), https://www.nytimes.com/2021/10/21/t-magazine/laura-ashley-batsheva.html (accessed 21 July 2024).
25. Vanessa Thorpe, 'How the florals and frills of Laura Ashley came to define an era', *The Guardian* (16 September 2018), https://www.theguardian.com/business/2018/sep/16/how-laura-ashley-florals-and-frills-define-an-era (accessed 21 July 2024).
26. Lauretta Roberts, 'In history: a timeline of Laura Ashley', *TheIndustry.fashion* (14 April 2022), https://www.theindustry.fashion/in-history-a-timeline-of-laura-ashley/ (accessed 2 December 2023).
27. Caroline Elenowitz-Hess, 'Reconstructing the "femme-fleur": floral modernism in the work of Madeleine Vionnet and Jeanne Lanvin', *Journal of Design History*, vol. 35, no. 2 (2021), pp. 99–117, https://doi.org/10.1093/jdh/epab035 (accessed 6 June 2024).
28. Entwistle 2000.
29. Ana Mendieta, 'Flowers on Body (Silueta Series)', *LadyKflo.com* (24 September 2021), https://ladykflo.com/flowers-on-body-silueta-series-by-ana-mendieta/ (accessed 2 April 2025).
30. D.J. Liberty, 'From cottagecore to tradwife: how retrofuturism in fashion predicts fascism', *Polyester* (17 December 2024), https://www.polyesterzine.com/features/from-cottagecore-to-tradwife-how-retrofuturism-in-fashion-predicts-fascism (accessed 6 June 2024).
31. Evans 2003, pp. 9–13.
32. Wilson 1985.
33. Hollander 1993.

Horrockses Fashions and Royal Style
Matthew Storey

1. Styles 2017, p. 457.
2. Staniland 1997, p. 120.
3. See https://player.bfi.org.uk/free/film/watch-royal-visit-to-messrs-horrockses-factory-1913-online (accessed 18 December 2025).
4. Boydell 2010, p. 135.
5. 'Sunshine clothes for sunny lands', *Picture Post* (8 February 1954), p. 26.
6. Ibid.
7. 'Copy Her Majesty…', *Daily Telegraph Women's Magazine* (Thursday, 20 May 1954), Sydney, Australia, p. 19.
8. Winefride Jackson, 'The Queen does not mind seeing the same dress on someone else', *Daily Telegraph* (22 December 1955). Horrockses Press Book, Lancashire Archives, DDHS/49/2.
9. Boydell 2010, p. 135.
10. Breward and Wood 2012, p. 43.
11. Boydell 2010, pp. 31–41.
12. Ibid., pp. 159–61.
13. Ibid., pp. 95–98.
14. *Sunday Mirror* (12 March 1967), no. 204, front page.
15. 'Hand-in-hand in the sun', *The People* (12 March 1967), p. 13.

Couture Connections: From Preston to Paris via London Scott Schiavone

1. Letter, Horrockses Fashions – 1951 Range, p. 2. Lancashire Archives, DDVC/ACC 7340.
2. 'Bride on a budget', British *Vogue* (May 1951), p. 124.
3. Letter from H. Mallot to Kathleen Molyneaux dated 2 May 1951. Lancashire Archives, DDVC/ACC 7340.
4. Jean Soward, 'At 33, he makes clothes for the Queen', *News Chronicle* (Tuesday 18 May 1954).
5. Ibid.
6. Ibid.
7. Meeting Minutes, 6 August 1951, p. 14. Lancashire Archives, DDVC/ACC 7340.
8. Sales Analysis 1950/1951, published 27 May 1951. Lancashire Archives, DDVC/ACC 7340.
9. Summary of Recommendations – Why Horrockses Fashions failed to meet delivery promises on the 1951 Spring range by W. Kerr, 1951. Lancashire Archives, DDVC/ACC 7340.
10. Ibid.
11. See Wilcox 2007, p. 60.
12. Meeting Minutes, 27 July 1949, p. 2. Lancashire Archives, DDVC/ACC 7340.
13. Meeting Minutes, 28 September 1949, p. 5. Lancashire Archives, DDVC/ACC 7340.
14. 'Eye catching but not functional', *LIFE* Magazine (1 December 1952), p. 71.
15. 'All an illusion but it's smart and popular', *Manchester Evening News* (May 1953).
16. 'Artist's model', *News Chronicle* (26 March 1953).
17. Dior 2015, p. 22.

SELECT BIBLIOGRAPHY

Atkinson, Harriet, *The Festival of Britain: A Land and its People* (London and New York, 2012)

Bide, Bethan, Jade Halbert and Liz Tregenza (eds), *Everyday Fashion: Interpreting British Clothing Since 1600* (London, 2024)

Bohm-Duchen, Monica (ed.), *Insiders/Outsiders: Refugees from Nazi Europe and their Contribution to British Visual Culture* (London, 2019)

Boydell, Christine, *Horrockses Fashions: Off-the-Peg Style in the '40s and '50s* (London, 2010)

Breward, Christopher, and Claire Wilcox (eds), *The Ambassador Magazine: Promoting Post-war British Textiles and Fashion* (London, 2012)

Breward, Christopher, and Ghislaine Wood, 'In the service of the state: change and continuity in design', in *British Design from 1948: Innovation in the Modern Age*, ed. Christopher Breward and Ghislaine Wood (London, 2012), pp. 40–63

Burger, Alissa, *The Television World of Pushing Daisies: Critical Essays on the Bryan Fuller Series* (Jefferson, NC, 2011)

Cotton, Michelle (ed.), *Nigel Henderson & Eduardo Paolozzi: Hammer Prints Ltd, 1954–75* (Firstsite, Colchester, exh. cat., 2013)

Council of Industrial Design, *Design '46: Survey of British Industrial Design as Displayed at the 'Britain Can Make It' Exhibition* (Victoria and Albert Museum, London, exh. cat., 1946)

De la Haye, Amy, *Ravishing: The Rose in Fashion* (The Museum at the Fashion Institute of Technology, New York, exh. cat., 2020)

Dior, Christian, *Dior by Dior: The Autobiography of Christian Dior*, trans. Antonia Fraser, (London, 2015)

Ehrman, Edwina, and Amy de la Haye, *London Couture: British Luxury 1923–1975* (London, 2015)

Entwistle, Joanne, *The Fashioned Body: Fashion, Dress and Modern Social Theory* (Cambridge, 2000)

Evans, Caroline, *Fashion at the Edge: Spectacle, Modernity, and Deathliness* (New Haven and London, 2003)

Gallery of English Costume, Platt Hall, *British Cotton Couture 1941–1961* (Manchester, 1985)

Gipson, Ferren, *Women's Work: From Feminine Arts to Feminist Art* (London, 2022)

Hlaváčkova, Konstantina, *The Mad Silkman: Zika & Lida Ascher, Textiles and Fashion* (Prague, 2019)

Hollander, Anne, *Seeing Through Clothes* (Berkeley, CA, 1993)

Jackson, Lesley, *Alastair Morton and Edinburgh Weavers: Visionary Textiles and Modern Art* (London, 2012)

Jackson, Lesley, *From Atoms to Patterns: Crystal Structure Designs from the 1951 Festival of Britain* (Wellcome Collection, London, exh. cat., 2012)

Juler, Edward, *Grown but Not Made: British Modernist Sculpture and the New Biology* (Manchester, 2016)

Klein, Bernat, *Eye for Colour* (London, 1965)

Llewellyn, Nigel, *The London Art Schools: Reforming the Art World, 1960 to Now* (London, 2015)

Mackrell, Alice, *Coco Chanel* (London, 1992)

Maguire, Patrick J., and Jonathan M. Woodham (eds), *Design and Cultural Politics in Postwar Britain: The 'Britain Can Make It' Exhibition of 1946* (London and Washington, 1997)

Nyburg, Anna, *The Clothes on Our Backs: How Refugees from Nazism Revitalised the British Fashion Trade* (London and Chicago, 2020)

Pritchard, Sue, 'British textile design: the quest for a new aesthetic', in *Henry Moore Textiles*, ed. Anita Feldman (Aldershot, 2009), pp. 9–25

Roux, Jessica, *Floriography: An Illustrated Guide to the Victorian Language of Flowers* (Kansas City, MO, 2020)

Staniland, Kay, *In Royal Fashion: The Clothes of Princess Charlotte of Wales and Queen Victoria, 1796–1901* (London, 1997)

Steele, Valerie (ed.), *The Berg Companion to Fashion* (Oxford, 2010)

Styles, John, 'Trade, industry and empire', in *Enlightened Princesses: Caroline, Augusta, Charlotte, and the Shaping of the Modern World*, ed. Joanna Marschner (New Haven and London, 2017), pp. 453–57

Tregenza, Liz, *Wholesale Couture: London and Beyond, 1930–70* (London, 2023)

Whitmore, Lucie, and Bethan Bide (eds), *Fashion City: How Jewish Londoners Shaped Global Style* (Museum of London, Docklands, exh. cat., 2023)

Wilcox, Claire (ed.), *The Golden Age of Couture: Paris and London, 1947–57* (London, 2007)

Wilson, Elizabeth, *Adorned in Dreams: Fashion and Modernity* (London, 1985)

AUTHOR BIOGRAPHIES

Paige Blake is a designer from Cornwall with a BA in Illustration and an MA in Surface Pattern and Textile Design. Her focus is on feminist art history, femininity and visual culture, with the aim of inspiring reflection and contributing to greater awareness of women's rights and meaningful change for women.

Dr Christine Boydell taught at De Montfort University, Leicester, for 16 years. She has published widely on the history of twentieth-century fashion and textiles. She began her work on Horrockses Fashions in 2000 with the exhibition *Our Best Dresses* at the Fashion Museum Bath. In 2010 Dr Boydell curated *Horrockses Fashions: Off-the-Peg Style in the '40s and '50s* at the Fashion and Textile Museum, London, and produced a book with the same title.

Amber Butchart is a curator, historian and broadcaster who specialises in the cultural and political history of textiles, dress and design. Amber Butchart is the history consultant and resident historian for BBC One's *Great British Sewing Bee*. She has presented documentaries for TV and radio, including *A Stitch in Time* for BBC Four, an exploration of the lives of historical figures through the clothes they wore.

Nadine Coyne is a Preston-based vintage collector. She was born and raised in the Preston area and still lives locally. Nadine Coyne's passion for vintage fashion started in the late 1970s. She has collected and worn Horrockses Fashions for many years.

Lisa Mason is Assistant Curator of Modern & Contemporary Design at National Museums Scotland. Recent exhibitions include *Archie Brennan: Tapestry Goes Pop!*, at Dovecot Studios, Edinburgh (co-curated with Kate Grenyer), and *Bernat Klein: Design in Colour*, at National Museums Scotland, Edinburgh. Lisa Mason is Chair of the Dress and Textile Specialists.

Scott Schiavone is a fashion historian and decorative arts curator at The Harris Museum, Preston, where he cares for the Horrockses Fashions' collection, the largest collection of its kind in the UK. Scott Schiavone's research focuses on nineteenth- and twentieth-century British and French fashion, couture and the social histories embedded in dress.

Matthew Storey is a curator at Historic Royal Palaces, where he cares for the Royal Ceremonial Dress Collection. He curated *Royal Style in the Making* (2021), featuring the wedding dress of Diana, Princess of Wales, and *Dress Codes* (2025) at Kensington Palace. Matthew Storey has published on Georgian portraiture and gardens, the wardrobe of Queen Victoria, and LGBTQ+ inclusive practice in museums and heritage sites.

Dr Liz Tregenza is a fashion historian. She is a lecturer in Cultural and Historical Studies at London College of Fashion and runs her own vintage business. Dr Tregenza previously worked extensively in museums. Her book, *Wholesale Couture: London and Beyond, 1930–70*, was published with Bloomsbury in 2023.

ACKNOWLEDGEMENTS

This book has been a true labour of love and it would not have been possible without the kindness, belief and generosity of so many people.

It has been a genuine pleasure to collaborate with the contributors to this book. Christine Boydell, thank you for your continued support and encouragement; and Lisa Mason, Paige Blake, Matthew Storey, Liz Tregenza and Nadine Coyne, working with you has been an absolute privilege. Your insights and writing have enriched this project enormously. I would also like to thank Amber Butchart for her foreword. Her endorsement of this publication means a great deal to the team.

My thanks go to Scala Arts & Heritage Publishers, especially Anna Danby, who believed in the idea from the very beginning, and Claire Young, whose encouragement and support have carried me through every stage of this process. I am also hugely grateful to Linda Schofield for her thoughtful and expert copy-editing, and to Nic Carter who designed the most beautiful book.

I would like to sincerely thank the Paul Mellon Centre for Studies in British Art, the Friends of The Harris and The Harris Trust for their generous funding. Their support made this publication possible and I am deeply appreciative. To Simon Critchley, thank you for capturing the dresses so beautifully – your photographs bring them to life in ways I could only have hoped for.

I feel incredibly lucky to work alongside such a dedicated team at The Harris. My particular thanks go to James Arnold for giving me the confidence and the green light to pursue this project, to Gemma Burns for her tireless image research and to Joanne Waters for her care, precision and invaluable support in the library.

I would also like to acknowledge the past curators of The Harris and the donors who built the Horrockses Fashions' collection. Their vision and care have left an extraordinary legacy and it has been an honour to work with such a remarkable archive.

Thank you to the staff at Lancashire Archives for helping me access the Horrockses' material, and to Martin Pel at Brighton Museums for his generosity in sharing his knowledge and supporting my research.

A very special thank you goes to Georgina Ripley, who recognised my potential and whose mentorship has meant more than I can properly express.

And finally, to my mum, Myra, you would have absolutely loved this. This is for you.

Scott Schiavone

INDEX

Page numbers in *italic type* refer to pictures.

PICTURE CREDITS

Every effort has been made to acknowledge correct copyright of images where applicable. Any errors or omissions are unintentional and should be notified to the Publisher, who will arrange for corrections to appear in any reprints:

pp. 2, 4, 6–7, 8, 11, 12, 17, 18, 20, 21, 23, 25, 26, 28, 29, 31, 33, 34, 35, 37, 38, 41, 42, 43, 46, 47, 48, 55, 57, 59, 66, 70, 71, 73–94, 101, 106, 107, 108, 109, 111 (above), 113, 120, 126, 135, 139, 143, 145 (left), 147, 148, 153–62, 164, 172 (below), 176, 179, 181, 183, 184, 192: Photographs by Simon Critchley; pp. 16, 18: Private collection; pp. 19 (below), 50, 103, 104, 105, 126, 128, 129130, 131, 142 (right): Photographs by Keziah Porter; p. 36: Photographer unknown. Reproduced with permission of Maryse Addison; p. 40: Vogue © Norman Parkinson Estate / Iconic Images; p. 46: Reproduced with permission of the Wells family; pp. 17, 57, 60, 61, 62: © Estate Joyce Badrocke / Victoria and Albert Museum, London; p. 63: Reproduced by permission of the Warner Textile Archive, Braintree District Museum Trust (P736b); p. 64: © Estate Elsbeth Juda / Victoria and Albert Museum, London; p. 65 (above): © 2025 The Paolozzi Foundation / Licensed by DACS; p. 67: © Estate Daphne Razzle / Victoria and Albert Museum, London; p. 69 © Peter Ascher, Ascher Family Collection; pp. 96, 116 (left): Chronicle / Alamy; pp. 100, 110: Retro Ad Archives / Alamy; p. 101: INTERFOTO/Alamy; p. 102: F8 Archive / Alamy; p. 110 (below): PA Images / Alamy; p. 112: © 2025 The Estate of Ana Mendieta Collection, LLC/Licensed by DACS; p. 116 (right), 122: © Look and Learn/Bridgeman Images; pp. 117, 121: © Historic Royal Palaces; p. 118: The Times / News Licensing; p. 119: SuperStock / Alamy; p. 123: Anwar Hussein / Getty Images News; p. 124 (left): Photo by DALMAS / AFP via Getty Images; p. 124 (right): Hulton Royals Collection / Getty Images; p. 125: Image courtesy of Kerry Taylor Auctions; pp. 129, 140, 142 (left): Victoria and Albert Museum, London; p. 132: Popperfoto / Getty Images; p. 133: © Condé Nast Publications / Victoria and Albert Museum, London; p. 134: Hulton Archive / Getty Images; p. 136: © 2025 Association Willy Maywald / ADAGP, Paris and DACS, London; pp. 137, 138: Photographs by Scott Schiavone; p. 141: RMN-Grand Palais / image Ville de Paris / dist. Photo SCALA, Florence; p. 144: © Philippe Potier /Institut Pasteur; p. 145 (right): Photograph by George Mavrikos. Image courtesy of Kerry Taylor Auctions; p. 146: Image courtesy of Manchester City Galleries; p. 150: Photograph by John French, London, UK. © John French / Victoria and Albert Museum, London; p. 151: Photograph by John French, London, UK, 1956. © John French / Victoria and Albert Museum, London; pp. 166, 167, 169, 170, 171, 172 (above), 173, 174, 175: Photographs by Liz Tregenza and Nadine Coyne; Back cover: Photograph by Henry Clarke for Horrockses Fashions. © Henry Clarke, Musée Galliera, Paris / ADACP, Paris and DACS, London.

FRONT COVER: Strawberry print ensemble, *Homes & Gardens* (March 1954), p. 55.

BACK COVER: Photograph taken by Henry Clarke for Horrockses Fashions.

PAGE 2: Cotton sun dress with matching sleeveless bolero jacket, printed with plates of food such as cherry pie, apples and asparagus, Horrockses Fashions, *c.*1953. The Harris (2001.37).

PAGES 4 AND 192: Cotton sun dress with bands of green and white and printed floral pattern, Horrockses Fashions, *c.*1954. The Harris (2000.302).

PAGES 6–7: Sample sheets, Horrockses Fashions, 1956–59. The Harris (2011.114).

PAGE 176: Brown cotton cocktail dress with floral pattern, Horrockses Fashions, *c.*1956. The Harris (2013.16).

PAGE 179: Yellow cotton day dress with abstract black-and-white floral pattern, Horrockses Fashions, *c.*1951. Textile designed by Alistair Morton (2020.17.3); Grey-and-white cotton dress with loosely drawn floral pattern set within geometric bands, Horrockses Fashions, *c.*1951. Textile designed by Alistair Morton. (2020.17.2). The Harris.

PAGE 180: Yellow voile housecoat with puffed sleeves and wrap-around closure with ties, Horrockses Fashions, *c.*1951. The Harris (2016.12.17).

PAGE 183: Cotton cocktail dress with black-and-white abstract roses and matching bolero jacket lined in pink, Horrockses Fashions, *c.*1954. The Harris (2025.6).

PAGE 184: The Harris's Decorative Art Curator Scott Schiavone styling a Horrockses Fashions' dress on a mannequin.

PAGE 189: Cotton evening dress with vertical stripes of pink and black with blue leaves and pink dots, Horrockses Fashions, *c.*1948. The Harris (2025.6).

PAGE 190: Cotton shirtwaister dress in bright pink with mother-of-pearl buttons, Horrockses Fashions, *c.*1954. The Harris (2025.6).

First published in 2026 by
Scala Arts & Heritage Publishers Ltd
43 Great Ormond Street
London WC1N 3HZ, UK
www.scalapublishers.com
An imprint of B. T. Batsford Holdings Ltd.

In association with The Harris, Preston PR1 2PP
www.theharris.org.uk

Managing Editor at Scala Arts & Heritage Publishers Ltd: Claire Young
Edited by Linda Schofield
Designed by Nic Carter / edits.studio
Printed in China.

ISBN 978-1-78551-639-9
10 9 8 7 6 5 4 3 2 1

Scala is represented in UK and Europe by Abrams & Chronicle Books, 1st Floor, 22–24 Ely Place, London EC1N 6TE and 57 rue Gaston Tessier, 75166 Paris, France.
www.abramsandchronicle.co.uk
info@abramsandchronicle.co.uk

MIX
Paper | Supporting responsible forestry
FSC® C104723

The exhibition *Horrockses Fashions: Everyday Glamour & the Art of British Ready-to-Wear* at The Harris, Preston.

The HARRIS
Preston City Council
FRIENDS of the Harris
HARRIS Trust

This book is supported by a Publications Grant from the Paul Mellon Centre for Studies in British Art.

PAUL MELLON CENTRE *for Studies in British Art*